Beginning GraphQL

Fetch data faster and more efficiently whilst improving the overall performance of your web application

Brian Kimokoti

BIRMINGHAM - MUMBAI

Beginning GraphQL

Acquisitions Editor: Koushik Sen
Content Development Editors: Murtaza Haamid, Rutuja Yerunkar
Production Coordinator: Ratan Pote

First published: July 2018

Production reference: 1260718

Published by Packt Publishing Ltd.
Livery Place
35 Livery Street
Birmingham
B3 2PB, UK.

ISBN 978-1-78961-054-3

www.packtpub.com

`mapt.io`

Mapt is an online digital library that gives you full access to over 5,000 books and videos, as well as industry leading tools to help you plan your personal development and advance your career. For more information, please visit our website.

Why Subscribe?

- Spend less time learning and more time coding with practical eBooks and Videos from over 4,000 industry professionals
- Improve your learning with Skill Plans built especially for you
- Get a free eBook or video every month
- Mapt is fully searchable
- Copy and paste, print, and bookmark content

PacktPub.com

Did you know that Packt offers eBook versions of every book published, with PDF and ePub files available? You can upgrade to the eBook version at `www.PacktPub.com` and as a print book customer, you are entitled to a discount on the eBook copy. Get in touch with us at `service@packtpub.com` for more details.

At `www.PacktPub.com`, you can also read a collection of free technical articles, sign up for a range of free newsletters, and receive exclusive discounts and offers on Packt books and eBooks.

Contributors

About the Author

Brian Kimokoti is a software developer with Andela. He holds a bachelor's degree in computer science from the Multimedia University of Kenya. For the last 5 years, he has been developing applications in PHP, JavaScript, and Python. Brian is a regular tech blogger on different online platforms and aspires to gain more experience and skills to an engineering and architect level.

About the Reviewer

Sam Anderson is currently working as a web developer at Joi Polloi. He gained experience working his way up the ladder, having progressed from being a summer intern to a web developer at ARM.

He completed his Master of Engineering degree at the University of Southampton. You can find out more about Sam on his LinkedIn profile: samanderson-00aa7222/.

Packt Is Searching for Authors like You

If you're interested in becoming an author for Packt, please visit `authors.packtpub.com` and apply today. We have worked with thousands of developers and tech professionals, just like you, to help them share their insight with the global tech community. You can make a general application, apply for a specific hot topic that we are recruiting an author for, or submit your own idea.

Table of Contents

Preface

Over-fetching and under-fetching data can negatively impact the performance of your web application. Future-proof your API structure and handle key development requirements by correctly defining types and schemas in GraphQL.

Though fairly new, GraphQL is quickly rising in popularity when it comes to API development. This book will teach you everything you need to know to start building efficient APIs with GraphQL. You'll begin by learning to create a simple scaffold application using Node.js and Express. Then, you'll explore core GraphQL concepts and study how GraphQL integrates with other frameworks in real-life business applications. By the end of the book, you will be able to successfully create efficient client-server REST-like applications.

Who This Book Is For

This book is ideal for developers who want to broaden their understanding of API development. Prior experience to JavaScript is required, with any prior work with React or Node.js being beneficial.

What This Book Covers

Chapter 1, *Understanding GraphQL Concepts*, covers an introduction to GraphQL and its advantages over REST, key concepts of GraphQL, and the construction of queries based on the structure of the data. It also teaches us how to create a simple GraphQL application and test the functionalities of our server using GraphiQL.

Chapter 2, *Querying Real-Time Data*, deals with real-time server response using GraphQL subscriptions. It also covers using Graphcool to implement GraphQL queries with ease. Finally, it explores the different entities of a GraphQL application and the fundamental concepts of writing queries and mutations in different ways.

Chapter 3, *Integrating GraphQL with Server-Side Applications Using the Apollo Client*, demonstrates the creation of interactive UIs and the integration of GraphQL functionality into a React application using Apollo Client, react-apollo, and other packages. It also covers working of the client cache, connecting components to retrieve data from the cache, updating the cache, and including optimistic UI.

To Get the Most out of This Book

For successful completion of this book, you will require a computer with at least 64-bit operating system, 4 GB RAM (minimum), and a stable internet connection.

The software required are macOS / Linux (Preferably Ubuntu 16.04) / Windows OS (Windows 7 minimum) and Visual Studio Code IDE.

Download the Example Code Files

You can download the example code files for this book from your account at www.packtpub.com. If you purchased this book elsewhere, you can visit www.packtpub.com/support and register to have the files emailed directly to you.

You can download the code files by following these steps:

1. Log in or register at www.packtpub.com.
2. Select the **SUPPORT** tab.
3. Click on **Code Downloads & Errata**.
4. Enter the name of the book in the **Search** box and follow the onscreen instructions.

Once the file is downloaded, please make sure that you unzip or extract the folder using the latest version of:

- WinRAR/7-Zip for Windows
- Zipeg/iZip/UnRarX for Mac
- 7-Zip/PeaZip for Linux

The code bundle for the book is also hosted on GitHub at https://github.com/TrainingByPackt/Beginning-GraphQL. In case there's an update to the code, it will be updated on the existing GitHub repository.

We also have other code bundles from our rich catalog of books and videos available at https://github.com/PacktPublishing/. Check them out!

Conventions Used

There are a number of text conventions used throughout this book.

CodeInText: Indicates code words in text, database table names, folder names, filenames, file extensions, pathnames, dummy URLs, user input, and Twitter handles. Here is an example: "Inside server.js, create a minimal express application with a single endpoint, graphql. This application gives a simple response when we navigate to localhost:3500/graphql."

A block of code is set as follows:

```
type Query
{
  getAuthors: [Author]
}
```

Any command-line input or output is written as follows:

```
$ prisma local start
```

Bold: Indicates a new term, an important word, or words that you see onscreen. For example, words in menus or dialog boxes appear in the text like this. Here is an example: "click on the **CREATE BOOK** button:"

Activity: These are scenario-based activities that will let you practically apply what you've learned over the course of a complete section. They are typically in the context of a real-world problem or situation.

 Warnings or important notes appear like this.

Get in Touch

Feedback from our readers is always welcome.

General feedback: Email feedback@packtpub.com and mention the book title in the subject of your message. If you have questions about any aspect of this book, please email us at questions@packtpub.com.

Errata: Although we have taken every care to ensure the accuracy of our content, mistakes do happen. If you have found a mistake in this book, we would be grateful if you would report this to us. Please visit www.packtpub.com/submit-errata, selecting your book, clicking on the Errata Submission Form link, and entering the details.

Piracy: If you come across any illegal copies of our works in any form on the Internet, we would be grateful if you would provide us with the location address or website name. Please contact us at copyright@packtpub.com with a link to the material.

If you are interested in becoming an author: If there is a topic that you have expertise in and you are interested in either writing or contributing to a book, please visit authors.packtpub.com.

Reviews

Please leave a review. Once you have read and used this book, why not leave a review on the site that you purchased it from? Potential readers can then see and use your unbiased opinion to make purchase decisions, we at Packt can understand what you think about our products, and our authors can see your feedback on their book. Thank you!

For more information about Packt, please visit packtpub.com.

Understanding GraphQL Concepts

GraphQL is a query language developed by Facebook for internal uses and was later open sourced. It performs the same functions as REST, however since it is a query language, it provides you with more control over the data that is to be fetched.

Similar to how SQL queries work while fetching the data from the RDBMS systems, GraphQL queries can be used to obtain just the required amount of data from the APIs.

GraphQL brings several advantages to the table including allowing clients to request only what they want, such as single endpoints, faster request-response cycles, and strong typing. GraphQL allows developers to define their data requirements and structure using types and schemas. They also define how to interact with the data by creating, updating, deleting, and fetching it using queries and mutations.

By the end of this chapter, you will be able to:

- Describe what GraphQL is and differentiate it from REST
- Set up and structure a simple GraphQL server application
- Test the GraphQL application by issuing queries using GraphiQL

Users have an additional advantage of getting the data in real-time by use of subscriptions provided by Apollo GraphQL and other developer communities like Graphcool. For more information about Apollo GraphQL, please visit the following website:
https://www.apollographql.com/
To check out Graphcool, please visit: https://www.graph.cool/.

In this chapter, we dive into different GraphQL concepts with practical implementations. We will begin by setting up a minimal Express application and gradually integrate GraphQL implementations while learning different concepts.

GraphQL Features

GraphQL has some clear advantages over REST, especially when it comes to some of the features mentioned in GraphQL as follows:

- **Hierarchical queries**: The structure of the queries look exactly like the response data. A client defies what response they want and what it should look like and the response data will automatically resemble what the client requested.
- **Introspective:** GraphQL allows the client to inquire about the fields, types, and supported queries. This is what allows GraphQL to perform query autocompletion and provide schema documentation. With this feature, the client can know exactly what operations are supported and the fields required and what sort of results can be returned. From that bulk information, the client can then carefully choose only the relevant parts.
- **Strongly typed**: The presence of a type system allows for syntactic query validation and the server responds with appropriate error messages. This implies that, if the schema on the server defies that it is expecting a query parameter to be an integer, a different data type will result in a validation error. Most GraphQL query editors have been equipped with the ability to detect these errors based on the schema.
- **Client-specified queries**: The client decides what data they want through different fields in the queries. This is a huge advantage over REST, where the GET function retrieves all the data from the API.

Setting up a Simple GraphQL Application

In this section, we are going to set up a GraphQL application by executing various stages. Let's begin by creating an Express application.

Creating an Express Application

This is a simple Node.js server application using Express. We will require an installation of Node.js on our respective platforms which is bundled with **Node Package Manager** (**npm**). We will also install YARN, an alternative and faster package manager compared to npm. We will also install nodemon, a utility that will watch our files and automatically restart our server. This saves us time not having to manually restart our application every time we need to, assuming that we already have Node.js installed.

Download link for Node.js: https://nodejs.org/en/download/.
Download link for YARN: https://yarnpkg.com/en/.
Download link for nodemon: https://nodemon.io/.

Creating a Directory Structure and Running the Express Application

Execute the following steps to create a directory structure for our application and running the Express application:

1. Run the following command to install YARN and nodemon globally:

```
$ npm install yarn nodemon -g # Globally install yarn and nodemon
```

2. Create a project folder, and inside the folder we will initialize a Node.js application. We will also need a body-parser and a middleware that parses client request bodies.

3. Type the following commands:

```
# Create project folder and navigate into the folder
$ mkdir GraphQL-Project && cd $_
# Create a server folder inside the project folder
$ mkdir server && cd $_
# Initializing an application. Will prompt for some answers.
$ yarn init
$ yarn add express@^4.9.8 body-parser@^1.9.3
$ touch server.js # Create main project file.
```

At this point, we should have the following folder structure:

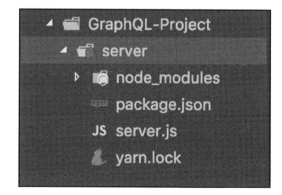

4. Inside `server.js`, create a minimal Express application with a single endpoint, `graphql`. This application gives a simple response when we navigate to `localhost:3500/graphql`. Take a look at this code:

```
const express = require('express'); // Require express module
const PORT = 3500; // Server port
const app = express(); // Create an express application
app.use('/graphql', (req, res)=> { // Add a route handler
  res.send( Welcome to Our Authors App");
});
app.listen(PORT, ()=> {
  console.log("Server Running on Port:", PORT);
});
```

5. Update the `package.json` file with scripts to run our application:

```
...
"scripts": {
  "start": "nodemon server.js"
}
...
```

 With the help of preceding commands, we only need to start our server once by running `npm start` or `yarn start`, and the server will restart any time we make changes to our code.

6. Run the server and make a request that return results:
   - Start the server with either `yarn start` or `npm start`.
   - Navigate to a browser window (preferably Google chrome) with the address `http://localhost:3500/graphql`. The browser should show **Welcome to Our Author's App**.

Schemas and Types

Just like database schemas, GraphQL schemas define the structure of our data. This includes the type of data and the kind of operations that can be performed on the data. Consider the following schema that uses the GraphQL query language to define an author:

```
type Author {
  id: ID!
  info: Person
}
```

```
type Person {
  name: String!
  age: Int
  gender: String
}
```

 The preceding schema remotely resembles an SQL schema that has tables `Author` and `Person` where the info field links to table `Person` using a foreign key. The difference is that SQL queries databases while GraphQL queries GraphQL APIs.

Even without prior knowledge, it's easy to work out what the preceding schema means. We are defining an author with the following fields:

- `id`: In GraphQL, type ID is used to indicate a unique identifier used to re-fetch data or as a key during caching. We will see this in practice at a later stage. The ID has a ! symbol after it; this indicates that it is required, which makes perfect sense to uniquely identify an author.
- `info`: The `info` field holds some common information about all authors, and we decided to abstract it to a separate type, `Person`. This kind of definition can be very handy in case we want to reuse a type.

Consider a situation where we must update our schema and include an `Editor`. Instead of redefining the same fields inside `Author` and repeating them in `Editor`, we simply reuse the type `Person` since the properties `name`, `age`, and `gender` are common for both `Author` and `Editor`.

GraphQL comes with a set of default scalar types, they are as follows:

- **Float:** A signed double precision floating point value, for example, `32.45`
- **Int:** A signed 32-bit integer, for example, `100`
- **String:** A sequence of characters encoded in UTF-8 for example, `Book`
- **Boolean:** `true` or `false`
- **ID:** Unique identifier that may be either an integer or string

In our example, we have utilized the preceding scalar types to implement our own custom types. We are also at liberty to define our custom scalar types by providing implementations of their serialization, deserialization, and validation.

Interfaces

Interfaces are abstract types that can be implemented by other types just like in many programming languages. Consider two types: `Person` and `Dog`; both require an `id` and a `name`. The two can implement an interface that has both fields and their own fields, too. Take a look at this code:

```
interface Shared {
  id: ID!
  name: String
}
type Dog implements Shared {
  did!
  name: String
  breed: String
}
type Person implements Shared {
  id: ID!
  name: String!
  height: Int
  age: Int
}
```

Resolvers

Resolvers are functions that provide the actual business logic implementation. The schema describes the structure of the queries, while the resolvers provide the actual functionality. In Apollo GraphQL, resolver functions take the following format:

```
fieldName(obj, args, context, info) { result }
```

- `fieldname`: Name of the resolver function which should match the field in the schema
- `obj`: Contains the result returned by the parent field
- `args`: Holds the arguments passed into the query
- `context`: Holds the pre-request state like authentication information that should be considered while resolving the query
- `info`: Contains information about the execution state of the query and should only be used in advanced cases

Queries that don't use arguments don't need to provide any of the aforementioned parameters. In the next section, we will see how all these fit together.

Queries

So far, all we have gone through is very theoretical concepts. In this section, we are going to add some flesh to our application and explore more concepts that require a more practical approach.

Queries are also part of the schema, but they have something special, as they are defined within type `Query`. These queries map to resolver functions so that when a query is received, it invokes a resolver function to do the heavy lifting. Queries define the fields, arguments, and result types. We are going to use a few tools from Apollo GraphQL:

- `graphql-tools`: Provides helper functions for stitching together the schema and the resolvers.
- `graphql-server-express`: Connects GraphQL to the Express server, as shown using in the following command:

  ```
  $ yarn add graphql-tools@^2.19.0 graphql-serverexpress@^1.3.3
  graphql@^0.12.3
  ```

Let's review the next section and update our code, which we will discuss in-depth afterwards.

Creating a GraphQL Server

Perform the following steps to create a GraphQL server:

1. Open the editor and copy-paste the following code:

    ```
    const express = require('express');
    const { graphqlExpress, graphiqlExpress } = require('graphql-
    server-express');
    const { makeExecutableSchema } = require('graphql-tools');
    const bodyParser = require('body-parser');
    ```

 For full code snippet, refer to `Code Snippets/Lesson 1` file.

2. Create some sample data:

```
const authors = [
{
  id: "1",
  info: {
    name: "Joe Kelly",
    age: 32,
    ...
  app.listen(PORT, ()=> {
  console.log("Server Running on Port:", PORT);
});
```

3. Save the file, and on the command line, use `npm start` and view the results in the browser using the URL `http://localhost:3500/graphiql`.

4. The browser should show the following windows:

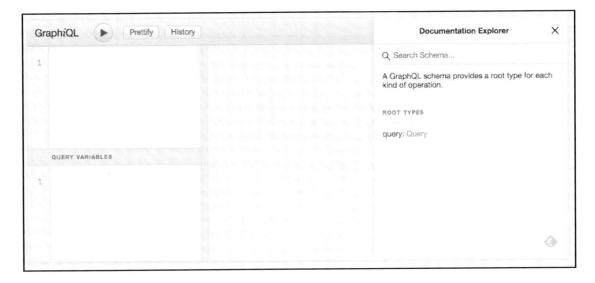

The following diagram shows the use of different parts of GraphiQL UI:

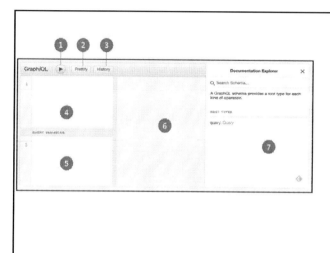

1. This button performs the operation.
2. This button will format our operation's appearance(indentation and spacing)
3. This button will show a history of operations on the left
4. This is where we write the actual operation: query, mutation, subscription etc.
5. This section is where we input variables, something we will look at later.
6. This section will show results of our operations.
7. This section shows the schema from our server

Let's see what the preceding code does. The first section is obvious; we import some packages that we have already discussed and then set up some sample data to use. The most interesting part is the three constants: const typeDefs, const resolvers, and const schema:

- const typeDefs: As discussed previously, this defines the schema. Inside the schema, we have a new type Query that defines an operation called getAuthors, which returns a list of objects of type Author. Since the query does not use any arguments, it does not need to supply any parameters:

```
type Query {
  getAuthors: [Author]
}
```

- const resolvers: Provide the actual implementation of the operations defined in the schema.
- const schema: We use makeExecutableSchema to map the schema operations to the appropriate resolver functions; getAuthors from const typeDefs is mapped to getAuthors from the Query object inside const resolvers.

We also have two endpoints defined. They are as follows:

- `graphql`: This is the main GraphQL endpoint. Any client application will make requests to this endpoint.
- `graphiql`: Serves an interactive graphical interface that enables testing our application before developing the client. The preceding screenshot shows the GraphiQL interface. We will practically demonstrate the functions of each section of this interface as we proceed.

There are separate ways of querying for data from our server, depending on our needs and structure of data. We can get all our authors using the following query:

```
query{
  getAuthors{
    info{
      name
      age
    }
  }
}
```

After running the query, the result should look like the following window:

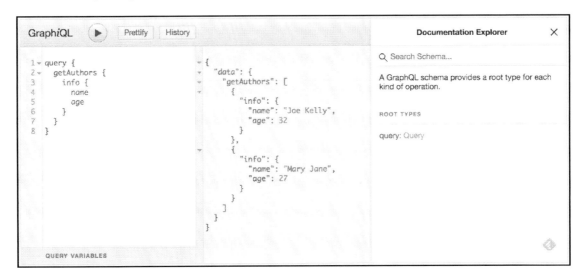

The operation is the same as making a GET request in REST to retrieve a list of authors but unlike in REST, we specify exactly what we want to be returned. We can do a variation of the query to get the name only.

In the preceding query, we get to specify what fields we want. Notice the structure of the result that resembles the query. If we wanted to get the author's name only, we would use the following query:

```
query {
  getAuthors {
    info {
      name
    }
  }
}
```

Now, we know that the first section is for writing queries while the second column shows the results.

Running a Query to Retrieve All Authors' Ages Only

Perform the following steps to run a query to only retrieve author's ages:

1. Navigate to the browser using the URL `http://localhost:3500/graphiql`.
2. Write the following query in the leftmost side of the window and press the Execute button:

```
query {
  getAuthors {
    info {
      age
    }
  }
}
```

The results should look like similar to the preceding diagram without the name field in the result.

Named Queries

The preceding query is file, but it would make even more sense if it didn't look so anonymous. We can give the query a name, which will make it easier to know what it is doing assuming the resolver function isn't so descriptive. We can rename our function in the schema and resolver from `getAuthors` to `k`, which is not very descriptive and would be difficult for client-side developers:

```
...
type Query {
  k: [Author]
}
`;

// The resolvers
const resolvers = {
  Query: {
    k: () => authors , // Resolver function name that's not descriptive.
...
```

Take a look at this screenshot:

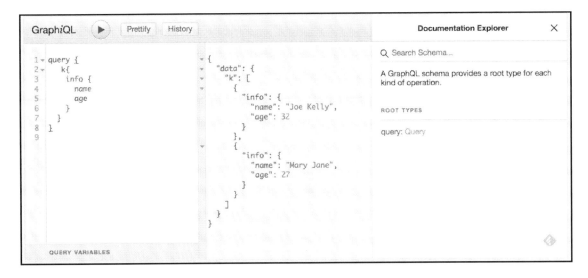

We can either change the query on the server or, even better, just name the query on our client side, and that will make it clear for everyone, as this screenshot shows:

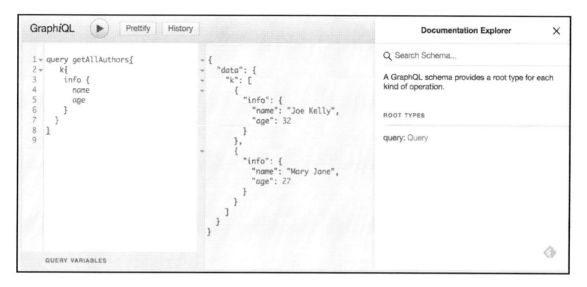

Arguments

To retrieve a single author would mean having a resolver function that takes a unique identifier, in our case, an ID. We will also pass an argument into our query on the client.

Since the queries are providing arguments, our resolver function will need to have at least two parameters. We also need to include the query as part of the schema.

The `retrieveAuthor` method returns a single author while `getAuthors` returns an array of authors, as indicated by the square brackets `[Author]`:

```
...
const typeDefs = `{
...
type Query {
getAuthors: [Author]
retrieveAuthor(id: ID!): Author
}
`;
const resolvers = {
  Query: {
    getAuthors: () => authors ,
    retrieveAuthor: (obj, { id }) =>
```

```
                authors.find(author => author.id === id)
        },
    };
    ...
```

We are using ES6 destructuring syntax to unpack the `id` from the `args` parameter. Alternatively, we can write the function as follows:

```
retrieveAuthor: (obj, args) => authors.find(author => author.id === args.id)
```

Take a look at this screenshot:

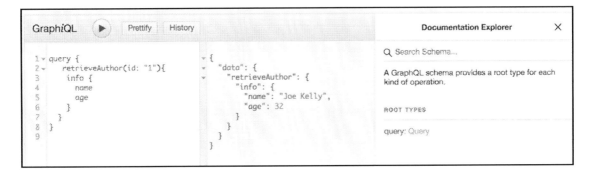

Variables

We can make the preceding query even more flexible and readable by avoiding the literal values. We can supply the arguments as variables, as shown in this screenshot:

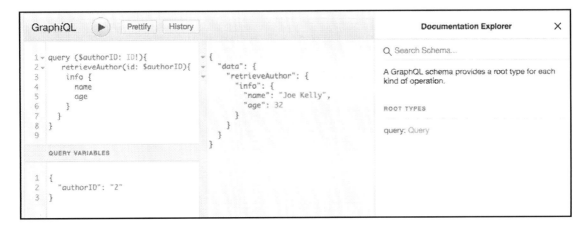

Query Aliases

Let's assume that we want to retrieve an author using their ID. This will return the fields we specified in the query, but what if we want to retrieve two authors at the same time? That would mean overlapping fields in the result. GraphQL does not permit directly querying for the same field with different arguments, as that would result in an error. Take a look at this screenshot:

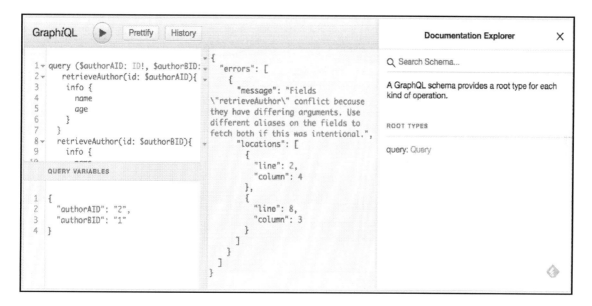

Aliases allow us to name the fields and get the results without conflict. Have a look at this screenshot:

```
GraphiQL    ▶    Prettify   History                                              < Docs

1▾ query ($authorAID: ID!, $authorBID: ID!){         ▾ {
2▾    author1: retrieveAuthor(id: $authorAID){        ▾   "data": {
3        info {                                       ▾     "author1": {
4          name                                               "info": {
5          age                                                  "name": "Mary Jane",
6        }                                                      "age": 27
7    }                                                        }
8▾    author2: retrieveAuthor(id: $authorBID){              },
9        info {                                       ▾     "author2": {
10         name                                               "info": {
11         age                                                  "name": "Joe Kelly",
12       }                                                      "age": 32
13   }                                                        }
14 }                                                        }
     QUERY VARIABLES                                       }
                                                          }
1  {
2    "authorAID": "2",
3    "authorBID": "1"
4  }
```

Fragments

In the preceding queries, we are repeating the same fields for both authors. We can avoid this by creating fragments on the returned type. This feature can be very useful, especially if we are retrieving many records. Look at this screenshot:

```
GraphiQL    ▶    Prettify    History                                      ⟨ Docs

1 ▾ query ($authorAID: ID!, $authorBID: ID!) {          ▾ {
2      author1: retrieveAuthor(id: $authorAID) {           "data": {
3        ...authorInfo                                        "author1": {
4      }                                                        "info": {
5      author2: retrieveAuthor(id: $authorBID) {                  "name": "Mary Jane",
6        ...authorInfo                                            "age": 27
7      }                                                        }
8    }                                                        },
9                                                           "author2": {
10 ▾ fragment authorInfo on Author {                         "info": {
11     info {                                                   "name": "Joe Kelly",
12       name                                                   "age": 32
13       age                                                  }
14     }                                                    }
15   }                                                    }
   QUERY VARIABLES                                      }

1  {
2    "authorAID": "2",
3    "authorBID": "1"
4  }
```

Equate the use of fragments to using functions in code to avoid rewriting functionality.

Using Inline Fragments

Identify and implement the fragments feature using inline fragments. Inline fragments are mostly used to retrieve data that may be different depending on certain conditions. For instance, getting a mode of transport that can either be an animal (legs) or a locomotive (wheels). The following query will return the name and either `numberOfLegs` or `numberOfWheels`, depending on whether the mode is an animal or a locomotive:

```
query ModesOfTransport {
  transportModes {
    name
    . . .
    on Animal{
      numberOfLegs
    }
    . . .
    on Locomotive{
      numberOfWheels
    }
  }
}
```

In this example, we are going to re-implement the fragments feature using inline fragments. Inline fragments are less flexible since they cannot be reused. The following example is not very suitable for inline fragments, since we only have one type, which is `Author`:

1. Update the `query` section to the following:

```
query ($authorAID: ID!) {
  retrieveAuthor(id: $authorAID) {
    ... on Author {
      info {
        name
        age
      }
    }
  }
}
```

2. Update the **QUERY VARIABLES** section to the following. Feel free to use any other ID for an author that exists:

```
{
   "authorAID": "2"
}
```

3. Run the query and observe the results, which should be in the following format:

```
1   query ($authorAID: ID!) {              {
2     retrieveAuthor(id: $authorAID) {        "data": {
3       ... on Author {                         "retrieveAuthor": {
4         info {                                  "info": {
5           name                                    "name": "Mary Jane",
6           age                                     "age": 27
7         }                                       }
8       }                                       }
9     }                                       }
10  }                                       }

QUERY VARIABLES

1   {
2     "authorAID": "2"
3   }
```

Directives

GraphQL provides two inbuilt directives that allow us to either include or skip some fields in our results.

The Skip Directive: @skip

We can retrieve our data but skip the `age` field for our first author if a `skipAge` variable is set to `true`.

Take a look at this screenshot (as you can see the age of `author1` is skipped from the result):

```
GraphiQL   ▶   Prettify   History                                    < Docs
1▾ query ($skipAge: Boolean!) {                    ▾ {
2▾   author1: retrieveAuthor(id: "1") {            ▾   "data": {
3       id                                         ▾     "author1": {
4       info {                                            "id": "1",
5         name                                            "info": {
6         age @skip(if: $skipAge)                           "name": "Joe Kelly"
7       }                                                 }
8     }                                                 },
9▾   author2: retrieveAuthor(id: "2") {            ▾     "author2": {
10      id                                                "id": "2",
11      info {                                            "info": {
12        name                                              "name": "Mary Jane",
13        age                                               "age": 27
14      }                                                 }
15    }                                                 }
16  }                                               }   }
    QUERY VARIABLES                                }

1  {
2    "skipAge": true
3  }                                                                    ◈
```

The Include Directive: @include

We can use the same technique to include the gender for our second author if an `includeGender` variable is set to `true`. Have a look at this screenshot:

```
GraphiQL   ▶   Prettify   History                                    < Docs
1▾ query ($skipAge: Boolean!, $includeGender: Boolean!) {    ▾ {
2▾   author1: retrieveAuthor(id: "1") {                       ▾   "data": {
3       info {                                                ▾     "author1": {
4         name                                                      "info": {
5         age @skip(if: $skipAge)                                     "name": "Joe Kelly"
6       }                                                           }
7     }                                                           },
8▾   author2: retrieveAuthor(id: "2") {                       ▾     "author2": {
9▾     info {                                                 ▾       "info": {
10        name                                                          "name": "Mary Jane",
11        age                                                           "age": 27,
12        gender @include(if: $includeGender)                           "gender": "F"
13      }                                                             }
14    }                                                             }
    QUERY VARIABLES                                            }   }
                                                              }
1  {
2    "skipAge": true,
3    "includeGender": true
4  }                                                                    ◈
```

Mutations

While Queries are synonymous to REST method that fetches data - GET, mutations are synonymous to REST methods that create and update data such as, POST, PUT, PATCH, and DELETE.

 You can equate write/update methods in REST to mutations in GraphQL.

Creating a New Author

We will create a new type in the schema under `Mutation` and a corresponding resolver to create a new author. We will design the mutation in the same manner that an author name and gender must be provided. Let's examine the following code:

```
...
type Mutation {
  createAuthor(name: String!, gender: String!) : Author
}
`;
// The resolvers
const resolvers = {
...
,
Mutation: {
  createAuthor: (obj, args) => {
    const id = String(authors.length+1); // Generate new author id
    const { name, gender} = args;
    const newAuthor = {
      id,
      info: {
        name,
        gender
      }
    }
    authors.push(newAuthor);
    return newAuthor;
  }
 }
};
...
```

Take a look at this screenshot:

Now, let's update the query and variable sections.

Navigate to the browser using the URL `http://localhost:3500/graphiql`. Update the query and variables sections as follows:

```
// Query section
mutation createNewAuthor($authorName: String!, $authorGender: String!) {
  createAuthor(name: $authorName, gender:$authorGender) {
    ...
    authorInfo
  }
fragment authorInfo on Author {
  id
  info {
    name
    age
    gender
  }
}
// Variables section.
{
  "authorName" : "Margie Chen'g",
  "authorGender": "F"
}
```

You can replace these names with any names of your choice.

Execute the query, which should return results similar to the following:

```
1  mutation createNewAuthor($authorName: String!, $authorGender: {
2    createAuthor(name: $authorName, gender: $authorGender) {        "data": {
3      ...authorInfo                                                   "createAuthor": {
4    }                                                                   "id": "3",
5  }                                                                     "info": {
6                                                                          "name": "Margie Chen'g",
7  fragment authorInfo on Author {                                         "age": null,
8    id                                                                    "gender": "F"
9    info {                                                              }
10     name                                                            }
11     age                                                           }
12     gender                                                      }
13   }
14 }
15

QUERY VARIABLES

1  {
2    "authorName" : "Margie Chen'g",
3    "authorGender": "F"
4  }
```

Updating an Author

We can now update our created author. Since it's updating an existing record, the only
required field is the author ID. We can add a custom error to be shown if the author is not
found:

```
...
type Mutation {
  createAuthor(name: String!, gender: String!) : Author,
  updateAuthor(id: ID!, name: String, gender: String, age: Int): Author
...
  throw new Error('Author ID not found');
      }
    }
  }
}
...
```

For full code snippet, refer to `Code Snippets/Lesson 1` file.
The preceding code gets an author from the array of authors and updates their details before returning the author information. If the ID supplied is not found, an error is thrown, which will show on the client side. The implementation is very similar as creating an author.

Take a look at this screenshot:

```
GraphiQL    ▶    Prettify    History                                      ⟨ Docs

1 ▾ mutation updateAuthor($authorID: ID!, $name: String!, $gender: String!, $age: Int) {   ▾ {
2      updateAuthor(id: $authorID, name: $name, gender: $gender, age: $age) {        "data": {
3        ...authorInfo                                                                 "updateAuthor": null
4      }                                                                             },
5   }                                                                             ▾ "errors": [
6                                                                                 ▾   {
7 ▾ fragment authorInfo on Author {                                                     "message": "Author ID
8      id                                                                       not found",
9 ▾    info {                                                                   ▾      "locations": [
10       name                                                                           {
11       age                                                                              "line": 2,
12       gender                                                                           "column": 3
13     }                                                                                }
14   }                                                                                ],
    QUERY VARIABLES                                                                 "path": [
1 ▾ {                                                                                  "updateAuthor"
2      "name": "Margie Chen'g",                                                      ]
3      "gender": "F",                                                            }
4      "authorID": "",                                                         ]
5      "age": 23                                                           }
6   }
```

Let's use the following code snippet to update the author information:

```
mutation updateAuthor($authorID: ID!, $name: $String!, $gender: String!,
$age: Int) {
  updateAUthor(id: $authorID, name: $name, gender: $gender, age: $age) {
    ...
    authorInfo
  }
}
fragment authorInfo on Author {
  id
  info {
    name
    age
    gender
  }
}
```

An error is thrown, since we did not provide an author ID, and the same would happen if we provided an ID that does not exist. We can now make a valid mutation to update the name of an existing author.

Let's examine the following screenshot:

```
GraphiQL  ▶  Prettify  History                                                      < Docs
 1 ▾ mutation updateAuthor($authorID: ID!, $name: String!, $gender: String!, $age: Int) {
 2       updateAuthor(id: $authorID, name: $name, gender: $gender, age: $age) {
 3           ...authorInfo
 4       }
 5   }
 6
 7 ▾ fragment authorInfo on Author {
 8       id
 9 ▾     info {
10           name
11           age
12           gender
13       }
14   }
   QUERY VARIABLES

 1 ▾ {
 2       "name": "Margaret Chen",
 3       "gender": "F",
 4       "authorID": "3",
 5       "age": 23
 6   }
```

```
▾ {
    "data": {
      "updateAuthor": {
        "id": "3",
        "info": {
          "name": "Margaret Chen",
          "age": 23,
          "gender": "F"
        }
      }
    }
  }
```

Since we are using memory storage in our application, if we create an author and edit the code, the new author will be erased, and we will have to create the record afresh.

Since we are using named queries, we can always check our history by clicking on the **History** button and reuse a query with some minor edits instead of retyping a whole query:

Activity: Including Delete Operations in Our Application

Now that we have learned how to implement different queries and mutations, we are going to use that knowledge and update our existing application to include a delete operation.

Scenario

Imagine the authors are part of an organization and one of the authors decides to leave. You are required to implement a method that will delete the author from the system.

Aim

The aim of this activity is to get hands-on with queries and mutations.

Steps for Completion

1. Update the schema to include a `DeleteMessage` type that returns the `Id:ID!` of the deleted author and a `message: String`:

```
type DeleteMessage {
  id: ID!,
  message: String
}
```

2. Update the schema to include a `deleteAuthor` mutation that takes an `Id:ID!` as the argument and returns `DeleteMessage`:

```
type Mutation {
  ...
  deleteAuthor(id:ID!): DeleteMessage
}
```

3. Create a resolver method for the delete method created in the schema. The resolver method should check if the author by the given ID exists and delete them; otherwise, it should return an error that states `Author ID not found`:

```
const resolvers = {
  deleteAuthor: (obj, { id, name, gender, age}) => {
    const author = authors.find(author => author.id === id);
    if(author) {
      const authorIndex = authors.indexOf(author);
      authors.splice(authorIndex, 1);
      return { id, message: `Author with Id ${id} deleted
      successfully` }
    } else {
      throw new Error('Author ID not found');
    }
  }
}
```

4. Ensure that the server is running and navigate to the browser using the URL `http://localhost:3000/graphiql` and test out the functionality. Take a look at this screenshot:

```
1▾ mutation deleteAuthor($authorID: ID!) {
2      deleteAuthor(id: $authorID) {
3        id
4        message
5      }
6  }
```
QUERY VARIABLES
```
1  {
2      "authorID": 1
3  }
```

```
▾ {
▾   "data": {
      "deleteAuthor": {
        "id": "1",
        "message": "Author with Id 1 deleted successfully"
      }
    }
  }
```

 Trying to delete the author again will result in an error.

Take a look at this screenshot:

```
1▾ mutation deleteAuthor($authorID: ID!) {
2      deleteAuthor(id: $authorID) {
3        id
4        message
5      }
6  }
```
QUERY VARIABLES
```
1  {
2      "authorID": 1
3  }
```

```
▾ {
    "data": {
      "deleteAuthor": null
    },
▾   "errors": [
▾     {
        "message": "Author ID not found",
        "locations": [
          {
            "line": 2,
            "column": 3
          }
        ],
        "path": [
          "deleteAuthor"
        ]
      }
    ]
  }
```

GraphQL.js

All of the preceding implementation is based on tools that have been created by the Apollo community. Here's a sample sketch snippet demonstrating use of GraphQL.js and `express-graphql` by Facebook. The implementation is very similar and easy to understand:

```
$ yarn add graphql@^0.12.3 express-graphql@^0.6.12
const express = require('express');
const graphqlHTTP = require('express-graphql'); // Using expressgraphql
const { buildSchema } = require('graphql'); // Using GraphQL.js
const schema= buildSchema(`type Query { hello: String }`);
const rootResolver = { hello: () => 'Hello world!' };
const app = express();
app.use('/graphql', graphqlHTTP({
 schema: schema,
 rootValue: rootResolver,
 graphiql: true
})));
app.listen(4000, ()=> {
 console.log('Server running on port 4000');
});
```

If we paste the preceding code into a file named `index.js`, we can run the application using node `index.js` and access the application in our browser using the URL `http://localhost:4000/graphiql`.

This is an alternative way of implementing a GraphQL server. The structure is pretty much the same as using Apollo GraphQL. This is also not part of the application we are creating and should be set up independently. The code for the application we are building should be preserved for future use.

Summary

In this chapter, we have introduced ourselves to GraphQL, its differences with REST, and learned how to set up a server using GraphQL using packages from the Apollo community. We have also created a simple GraphQL application and tested different concepts using GraphiQL. We have also briefly seen an alternative way of creating a GraphQL server using GraphQL.js. All this has been achieved by building a GraphQL application.

In the next chapter, we will continue building on the current application and include real-time data using subscriptions. We will also explore different packages by Graphcool which will diversify our knowledge on other ways of implementing GraphQL.

2
Querying Real-Time Data

In the previous chapter, we introduced ourselves to GraphQL, its differences with REST, and how to set up a server using GraphQL, using packages by the Apollo community. We have also created a simple GraphQL application and tested different concepts using GraphiQL. We have also briefly seen an alternative way of creating a GraphQL server using GraphQL.js. All of this has been achieved by building along a GraphQL application.

In this chapter, we are going to focus on how we can make our server respond to requests in real time. We will also look at third-party development tools by Graphcool that have made learning and implementation of GraphQL very easy.

 Using WebSockets, Apache Kafka, Fanout/Pushpin, and so on, are the common ways of getting real-time data in web applications.

By the end of this chapter, you will be able to:

- Implement real-time functionality using subscriptions
- Explain some of the most common tools being developed by different developer communities apart from Apollo
- Identify the different ways of protecting APIs by adding authentication

Real-Time Query Processing

Real-time data querying has become the need of the hour. By processing the data in real time, we can gain easy and real-time insights into the data. Real-time query processing also facilitates affordability by providing insights into the data instantly rather than having to store, process, and then gain insights from it.

Weather station data like humidity and temperature, chat applications, and so on, are the example applications that require real-time data.

Before we proceed, our single file is becoming pretty big and messy, and it will be a good practice to do some refactoring. We will create three different files under the `server` directory, alongside the existing `server.js` and move different sections from `server/server.js` to the respective files.

Perform the following steps to refactor the code to make it more readable:

1. Create a file named `author.js`, in the server directory.
2. Now, cut-paste the code for array of authors into this file:

```
//Sample data
const authors = [
{
  id: "1",
  info:
  {
    name: "Joe Kelly",
    age: 32,
    gender: "M",
  }
},
{
  id: "2",
  info:
  {
    name: "Mary Jane",
    age: 27,
    gender: "F",
}}];
module.exports = authors;
```

3. Create a file called `server/resolver.js`, and paste the code from `Chapter 1`, *Understanding GraphQL Concepts*, under the variable `resolvers`.
4. Create a `schema.js` file, and paste the code from `Chapter 1`, *Understanding GraphQL Concepts* under the `typeDefs` variable.

5. At this point, `server/server.js` should look as follows, with as little code as possible. Our main file is now small, manageable, less messy, and more readable:

```
const express = require('express');
const { graphqlExpress, graphiqlExpress } =
require('graphql-server-express');
const bodyParser = require('body-parser');
const schema = require('./schema');
const resolvers = require('./resolvers');
const PORT = 3500;
const app = express();
// The GraphQL endpoint
app.use('/graphql', bodyParser.json(), graphqlExpress({
schema }));
// GraphiQL, a visual editor for queries
app.use('/graphiql', graphiqlExpress({ endpointURL: '/
graphql' }));
app.listen(PORT, ()=>
{
  console.log("Server Running on Port:", PORT);
});
```

6. Navigate to the command line under the current project folder, and run the application using `npm start` or `yarn start`, depending on the package manager.

7. Navigate to the browser using the URL `localhost:3500/graphiql`.

The browser window should show a GraphiQL window similar to the following:

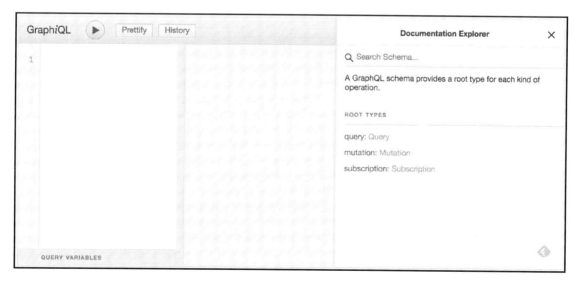

Subscriptions

Real-time applications are increasingly becoming the norm and most application developers are trying to achieve it. Real-time data added to the reduced size of GraphQL responses result in very fast applications that require very little bandwidth compared to REST. This feature is provided by Apollo GraphQL. Implement this feature for creating new authors to use subscriptions.

Hooking up PubSub

We need to create a PubSub object and pass in a topic that we can publish and subscribe to get new data. We will install graphql-subscriptions, which provides us with the PubSub class and updates resolver.js. Take a look at this code line:

```
$ yarn add graphql-subscriptions@^0.5.6
```

PubSub is a class that exposes a publish and subscribe API. It receives the publish command from the application logic and forwards it for execution in the GraphQL execution engine. PubSub also includes a mechanism that converts a specific PubSub event into a stream of AsyncIterator, which we can use with the GraphQL subscriptions resolver. AsyncIterator is an alternative lightweight implementation of streams in JavaScript. It takes a topic as an argument which we can publish data to.

Subscription resolvers are slightly different from query and mutation resolvers. A subscription resolver takes an object with a subscribe field and a subscription resolver method. The method must also return an AsyncIterator, which is provided by the asyncIterator method from PubSub. The code for the same is as follows:

```
const authors = require('./authors');
const { PubSub } = require('graphql-subscriptions');
const AUTHORS_TOPIC = 'newAuthor'; // Create a topic to subscribe/
publish to
const pubsub = new PubSub(); // Create Pubsub object
// The resolvers
const resolvers =
{
...,
  Subscription:
  {
  // Include Subscription in root resolver
    createAuthorWithSubscription:
    {
      // Subscription operation
```

```
      subscribe: () => pubsub.asyncIterator(AUTHORS_TOPIC) //
      Subscribe to topic
    }
  }
};
module.exports = resolvers;
```

We then need to publish to our topic when a new author is created. We will modify the
`createAuthor` resolver function to publish to the topic after creating a new author. The
code for the same is as follows:

```
...
createAuthor: (obj, args) =>
{
  const id = String(authors.length+1);
  const { name, gender} = args;
  const newAuthor =
  {
    id,
    info:
    {
      name,
      gender
    }
  }
  authors.push(newAuthor);
  pubsub.publish(AUTHORS_TOPIC, { createAuthorWithSubscription: newAuthor
}); // Publish new author
  return newAuthor;
},
...
```

By default, `graphql-subscriptions` exports an in-memory `EventEmitter`, event system
to rerun subscriptions but also supports external Pub/Sub systems that implement
`AsyncIterator`. The default implementation does not support sharing subscriptions and
publications across multiple servers. It is advisable to use alternatives such as `Redis
PubSub` (`graphql-redis-subscriptions`) or MQTT (`graphql-mqtt-subscriptions`) in
a production environment.

Adding Subscriptions to Schema

Subscription is just another GraphQL type like query and mutation, so we are going to create a root schema definition by updating `schema.js`. Update the `schema.js` file as follows:

```
...
const typeDefs = `
...
type Subscription
{
  createAuthorWithSubscription: Author
}
`
...
```

Configuring the Server to Use WebSocket

WebSocket is a technology that allows creation of an interactive session between the client and the server. It is event driven (actions are performed on defined events). Most chat applications rely on this technology to send messages in real time.

 Socket IO and `subscriptions-transport-ws` are the sample packages/libraries used to implement WebSockets.

`subscriptions-transport-ws` is a GraphQL WebSocket server and client to facilitate GraphQL operations over WebSocket. It creates a `SubscriptionServer` by taking in server options and WebSocket options as first and second parameters, respectively. The server options include `execute` and `subscribe` methods from the GraphQl package. The `execute` method evaluates requests and returns the execution result. The `subscribe` method yields a stream of execution results, representing the response stream.

We will now configure the server to use WebSocket so that we can import the real-time data to our app:

1. Since `subscriptions-transport-ws` is meant to work with the native HTTP package, we will wrap our express app inside an `http` method. We will also add a `subscriptionsEndpoint` to a GraphiQL endpoint to enable GraphiQL to communicate over `Websocket`.

 For the full code snippet, refer to `Code Snippets/Lesson 2` file.

Take a look at this code:

```
$ yarn add subscriptions-transport-ws
# Install the WebSocket server package
...
const { execute, subscribe } = require('graphql');
const { SubscriptionServer } = require('subscriptions-transport-
ws');
const { createServer } = require('http');
const PORT = 3500;
const app = express();
// The GraphQL endpoint
app.use('/graphql', bodyParser.json(), graphqlExpress({ schema }));

// GraphiQL, a visual editor for queries
app.use('/graphiql', graphiqlExpress({ endpointURL: '/graphql',
// Include a Websocket endpoint for GraphiQL
subscriptionsEndpoint: 'ws://localhost:${PORT}/subscriptions'
}));
var ws = createServer(app); // Wrap express app inside http
ws.listen(PORT, ()=>
{
  console.log("Server Running on Port:", PORT);
...
}, {
    server: ws,
    path: '/subscriptions',
  });
});
```

The server can now communicate over both normal HTTP and WebSocket connection. Mutation requests will be received via an HTTP connection, while the subscription responses will be sent over a WebSocket connection.

2. We can now test our functionality by opening two separate browser windows, one to run our subscription, while the other runs a mutation to create an author. The expected output will be as follows:

```
GraphiQL  ▶  Prettify  History                                          ‹ Docs

1 ▾ subscription {                          "Your subscription data will appear here after server
2 ▾   createAuthorWithSubscription {        publication!"
3        id
4 ▾      info {
5          name
6          age
7          gender
8        }
9      }
10 }

QUERY VARIABLES
```

The subscription server is waiting for a publish event to our specified topic. It will then push the published data to our client in real time.

3. We can make a `createAuthor` mutation, and the results will appear in the preceding window without having to refresh it. Take a look at this screenshot:

```
GraphiQL  ▶  Prettify  History                                          ‹ Docs

1 ▾ mutation createNewAuthor($authorName: String!, $authorGen ▾ {
2      createAuthor(name: $authorName, gender: $authorGender) ▾   "data": {
3        ...authorInfo                                              "createAuthor": {
4      }                                                              "id": "3",
5 }                                                                   "info": {
6                                                                       "name": "Brian Malack",
7 ▾ fragment authorInfo on Author {                                    "age": null,
8      id                                                              "gender": "M"
9 ▾    info {                                                        }
10       name                                                      }
11       age                                                     }
12       gender                                                }
13     }
14 }
15
QUERY VARIABLES

1  {
2     "authorName": "Brian Malack",
3     "authorGender": "M"
4  }
```

Following is the subscription window:

```
GraphiQL    ▶    Prettify    History                                        ⟨ Docs

1 ▾ subscription {                              ▾ {
2 ▾   createAuthorWithSubscription {            ▾    "createAuthorWithSubscription": {
3       id                                             "id": "3",
4 ▾     info {                                  ▾      "info": {
5         name                                            "name": "Brian Malack",
6         age                                             "age": null,
7         gender                                          "gender": "M"
8       }                                              }
9     }                                              }
10  }                                           }
```

Other Community Tools

GraphQL is becoming increasingly popular, and a lot of developer communities are developing tools and APIs to make working with it easier. Just like Apollo, the Graphcool community has also developed several awesome server-side tools, and we are going to look at some of the most common tools and their use cases.

GraphQL Playground

GraphQL Playground is a tool that is very similar to GraphiQL but with some additional features.

It utilizes GraphiQL components under the hood, but it is a more powerful query editor, enabling better development workflows. Some of the additional features include the following:

- **Automatic schema reloading**: The schema automatically reloads if any changes are made on the server application
- **Tabs**: Queries can be run in separate tabs

 There's a desktop version of GraphiQL that has been developed using Electron JS that supports most of the features provided by GraphQL Playground.

With the application in Chapter 1, *Understanding GraphQL Concepts* still running, we can input our server URL and run a query to fetch all authors:

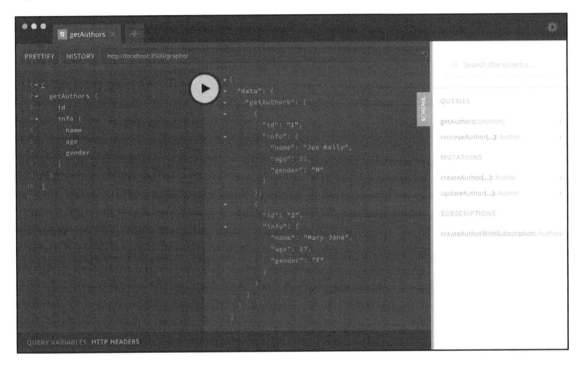

Use the following code snippet as illustrated in the preceding screenshot:

```
// Query
query
{
  getAuthors
  {
    id
    info
    {
      name
      age
      gender
    }
  }
}
```

graphql-yoga

If the whole concept of creating an express application, connecting it with HTTP, and configuring subscriptions manually seems too much, then `graphql-yoga` is the solution to your problem.

It is a complete GraphQL server that is easy to set up, has good performance, and provides great developer experience.

`graphql-yoga` is based on some great libraries that we have used in `Chapter 1,` *Understanding GraphQL Concepts*; they include these:

- `express/apollo-server`: It is an extensible web server framework that provides all functionalities provided by the `graphql-express-server`.
- `graphql-subscriptions`/`subscriptions-transport-ws`: This is a GraphQL subscriptions server.
- `GraphQL.js`/`graphql-tools`: These are GraphQL engine and schema helpers.
- `graphqlGraphql-playground`: This is an interactive query editor that shows when you navigate to the browser. This means you don't need to do any installation.

We will now implement a simple GraphQL server using `graphql-yoga`. It will hold simple string records and allow us to create, update, and fetch records. All we need is a simple project structure and to install one package.

Creating a Server Using graphql-yoga

Execute the following steps to create a server using `graphql-yoga`:

1. Let's execute the following commands to initialize a new application:

```
$ mkdir yoga && cd yoga # Create and navigate into project folder
$ yarn init # Answer prompts
$ yarn add graphql-yoga # Install graphql-yoga
$ touch server.js # Create main working file
```

 For full code snippet, refer to `Code Snippets/Lesson 2`.

2. Inside `server.js`, we will add the following code, which has a lot of similarities to those we saw in Chapter 1, *Understanding GraphQL Concepts*, but with fewer lines of code and configurations:

```
const { GraphQLServer } = require('graphql-yoga');
var records = [];
/* Create a GraphQL schema */
...
        throw Error(`Record Index Does not Exist`);
      }
      records[+recordIndex] = recordName;
      return `Record Updated to: ${records[recordIndex]}`;
    }
  }
};
// Create a GraphQL server using GraphQLServer
const server = new GraphQLServer({ typeDefs, resolvers });
server.start(() => console.log('Server is running on
localhost:4000'));
```

In the preceding code snippet, we have initialized a simple GraphQL schema, `typeDefs`, with one query (`fetchRecords`) and two mutation (`createRecord` and `updateRecord`) operations. We then created resolver functions for these operations and instantiated a server using `GraphQLServer` from `graphql-yoga`.

3. With the preceding setup, we can use GraphQL Playground to test out some of the highlighted functionalities by writing a query and clicking on the Play button. Start the application with `yarn start` or `npm run start`. Navigate to `http://localhost:4000` in `graphql-playground`. The default port for `graphql-yoga` is `4000`.

4. We can test out different queries and mutations as follows:

```
mutation createNewRecord {
    createRecord(recordData: "Cutlery")
}

query getRecords{
    fetchRecords
}

mutation updateRecords {
    updateRecord(recordIndex: 1, recordName: "Tools")
}
```

```
{
    "data": {
        "fetchRecords": [
            "Books",
            "Tools",
            "Cutlery"
        ]
    }
}
```

5. We can also use variables just as in GraphiQL. Take a look at this screenshot:

```
mutation createNewRecord($recordData: String!) {
    createRecord(recordData: $recordData)
}

query getRecords {
    fetchRecords
}

mutation updateRecord($index: Int!, $name: String!) {
    updateRecord(recordIndex: $index, recordName: $name)
}
```

```
{
    "data": {
        "fetchRecords": [
            "Cutlery",
            "Books"
        ]
    }
}
```

QUERY VARIABLES   HTTP HEADERS

```
{
    "recordData": "Utensils"
}
```

Trying to update a record with a non-existent index will result in an error.

Take a look at this screenshot:

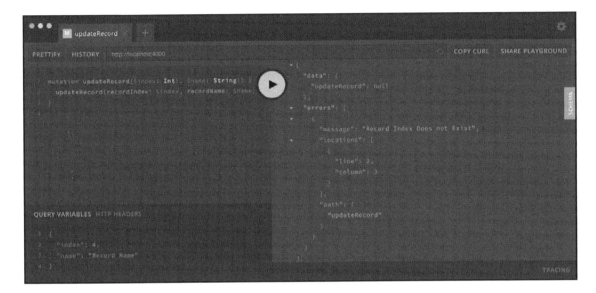

Use the following code for illustration:

```
mutation updateRecord($index: Int!, $name: String!)
{
  updateRecord(recordIndex: $index, recordName: $name)
}
```

Define the variables:

```
{
  "index":4,
  "name": "Record Name"
}
```

Subscriptions in graphql-yoga

Subscriptions are inbuilt in `graphql-yoga` and they need very minimal configuration to implement. Let's create an implementation for a subscription when a new record is created:

```
const { GraphQLServer, PubSub } = require('graphql-yoga'); //Require PubSub
var records = [];
const typeDefs = `
...,
...
...
  },
};
const pubsub = new PubSub();
const server = new GraphQLServer({ typeDefs, resolvers, context: { pubsub }
});
server.start(() => console.log('Server is running on localhost:4000'));
```

 For full code snippet, refer to `Code Snippets/Lesson 2` **file**.

The implementation is very similar to the previous application, except that we are passing in the `PubSub` instance as context. Take a look at this screenshot:

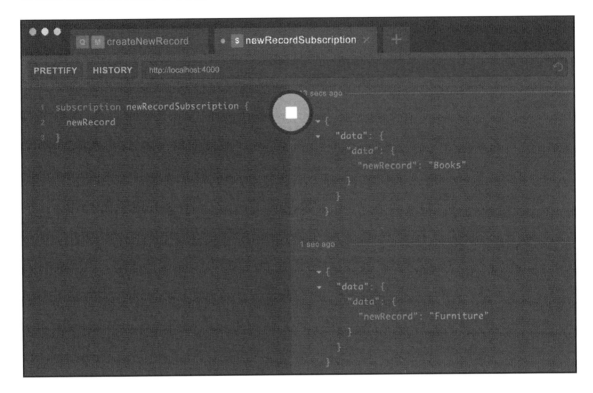

Use the following code and run it as illustrated:

```
subscription newRecordSubscription {
  newRecord
}
```

`graphql-yoga` uses port `4000` as the default port. To change the port and other options, you can pass in options in the `start` function, as shown here:

```
server.start({ port: 5000, endpoint: '/yoga',
subscriptions: '/yoga' }, ()=>
{
  console.log('Server is running on localhost:')
});
```

The Graphcool Framework

One of the tools developed by the Graphcool community is called the Graphcool Framework, an opinionated tool to develop serverless GraphQL backends. Graphcool turns your database into an API that you can consume directly. Currently, Graphcool only supports MySQL databases, but plans are in the pipeline to support other databases.

The Graphcool CLI is the command-line tool used to manage Graphcool services whose contents are defined in the `graphcool.yml` service definition file. The CLI offers tools to modify the local version of your service definition and file structure as well as syncing these changes with already deployed services.

Graphcool Services

Every Graphcool service consists of several components.

Type definitions contain the GraphQL Schema and are divided into two categories:

- **Model types**: Types that are to be stored in the database and are annotated with the `@model` directive and represent application entities:

```
type User @model
{
  id: ID! @isUnique # read-only (managed by Graphcool)
  # Optional system fields
  createdAt: DateTime! # read-only (managed by Graphcool)
  updatedAt: DateTime!
  name: String
}
```

- **Transient types**: Types that represent input or return types for API operations that and are not persisted in the database

Permission rules determine which users can use which operations. The following requires that a user be authenticated to create a todo:

```
permissions:
- operation: Todo.create
    authenticated: true
```

We can use the same rule for all operations under `Todo` by using a wildcard:

```
permissions:
- operation: Todo.*
    authenticated: true
```

Alternatively, we can include a query property that points to a file with a query that should return a Boolean. The following means that only authenticated users that satisfy the query in `Todo.graphql` can create a todo:

```
permissions:
- operation: Todo.read
  authenticated: true
  query: ./src/permissions/Todo.graphql
```

- **Functions**: Serverless functions that can react to events, extend API functionality, or act as hooks. Each function in the service definition file must have type and handler properties. The functions might have additional properties that are specific to the task they perform. Functions are categorized into three:
  - **Subscriptions**: Invoke functions based on events. A subscription function may be triggered when a new user is created to send them an email with a link to verify their account. Subscription functions need an additional query field which points to a file that contains a regular subscription query. Take a look at this code block:

    ```
    functions:
      emailNotification:
        type: subscription
        query: ./src/emailNotification.graphql
          handler:
            code:
              src: ./src/emailNotification.js
    ```

  - **Resolvers**: Resolvers add more functionality to the GraphQL schema by extending the existing CRUD API and are also used for authentication. Resolvers need an additional schema property that points to a file that extends the query or mutation type and additional types that we may need. The following is an example of a default resolver that is created when we initialize a new app with the Graphcool CLI. Take a look at this code block:

    ```
    functions:
    hello:
      handler:
        code: src/hello.js
      type: resolver
      schema: src/hello.graphql
    ```

    Each resolver can add a single query or mutation field to the GraphQL API, and this field takes in scalar arguments and returns a type that is specified in the same **Schema Definition Language** (**SDL**) document.

The limitation is that only one query or mutation field can be added and the input can only be a scalar type.

- **Hooks**: These execute before or after an API operation has been executed. They are mostly used to validate request data and format responses. Two types of hook points exist, `operationBefore` and `operationAfter`, and they are invoked before and after a write to the database, respectively. Hook functions need to specify an additional operation field that contains the model and specific database operation, for example, `User.create`. The following shows an example of an `operationBefore` hook that is executed before a user is created:

```
functions:
  validateAccount:
    type: operationBefore
    operation: User.create
    handler:
      webhook: http://example.org/email-validator
```

All of these three function types can call external APIs as handlers, in which case they use the webhook property under the handler:

- **Root tokens**: These are authentication tokens for API access as a list of strings that will be available when the service is deployed: `rootTokens: rootToken1` and `rootToken2`.

Creating a Graphcool Framework Application

Execute the following steps to create a Graphcool Framework application:

1. Creating a Graphcool Framework application requires the Graphcool CLI tool that we can install from npm:

```
$ npm install -g graphcool@0.11.5
```

2. We will initialize a new application with the following commands:

```
$ graphcool init graphcool-books # Create an app called graphcool-books
$ cd graphcool-books # Navigate into the app folder
```

3. We now have a simple default application with the following directory structure:

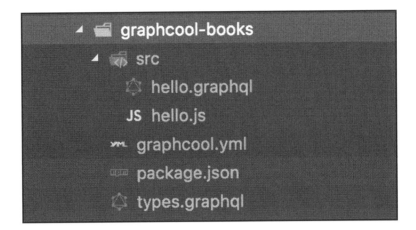

4. Take a look at this list:
   - `types.graphql`: Static GraphQL Schema definition using GraphQL SDL
   - `graphcool.yml`: Service configuration file
   - `hello.graphql`: Resolver function schema
   - `hello.js`: Actual resolver function to handle the logic

 For full code snippet, refer to `Code Snippets/Lesson 2` file.

5. We can update our schema definition in `types.graphql` to include a model for books, which has a many-to-one relation to the user. Take a look at this code block:

```
type User @model
{
  id: ID! @isUnique
  createdAt: DateTime!
...
...
  # Every relation also required a back-relation (to determine 1:1,
1:n or n:m)
  owner: User! @relation(name: "UserBooks")
}
```

This model will be synced with our database when we deploy our service. The `id`, `createdAt` (optional), and `updatedAt` (optional) fields are read-only fields managed by Graphcool.

Permission Management

Execute the following steps to include some permissions to control access to API information:

1. Let's update our permissions in `graphcool.yml` to the following:

```
...
permissions:
  - operation: "User.create"
...
...
    authenticated: true
    query: ./permissions/book.graphql
...
```

 For full code snippet, refer to `Code Snippets/Lesson 2` file.

Permissions for our relation (`UserBooks.connect`) have to be defined to allow a book to associate itself with an owner.

2. The permissions for the book node references `./permissions/book.graphql`, a query file that determines if the operations should happen or not by returning a Boolean value. There are some very specific rules guiding the whole process of writing permissions, permission queries, variables, and variable naming conventions. We can read further from the *Authorization, Permission Parameters,* and *Permission Queries* sections in the official documentation. Take a look at this:

```
$ mkdir permissions && cd permissions
$ touch book.graphql
```

3. Add the following to book.graphql:

```
query ($node_id: ID!, $user_id: ID!)
{
  SomeBookExists(
    filter:
    {
```

```
                id: $node_id,
                owner:
                {
                   id: $user_id
                }
            }
         )
      }
```

The query takes `user_id` for the authenticated user and the `node_id` for the node that's trying to access the permission. We then use a filter to determine if the `node/book` exists and that the currently authenticated user is the owner of that `node/book`.

Authentication

Since we have defined permissions, let us execute the following steps to set up a mode of authentication that will be used to enforce the permissions. Graphcool provides some already-built templates that we can easily integrate into our application.

1. We will add email/password authentication using the Graphcool CLI:

    ```
    $ graphcool add-template graphcool/templates/auth/email-password
    ```

    Take a look at this screenshot:

```
[64]    graphcool add-template graphcool/templates/auth/email-password
Downloading template graphcool/templates/auth/email-password from graphcool/templates ... ✔
The dependencies @types/bcryptjs, @types/validator, bcryptjs, graphcool-lib, graphql-request, validator have been
Written /Users/kimobrian/Desktop/Mapt/GraphQL-Course/packages/graphcool-books/package.json

yarn install v1.2.1
warning You are using Node "7.0.0" which is not supported and may encounter bugs or unexpected behavior. Yarn sup
|| ^5.7.0 || ^6.2.2 || ^8.0.0"
warning package.json: No license field
[1/4] Resolving packages...
[2/4] Fetching packages...
[3/4] Linking dependencies...
warning "graphql-playground-middleware-lambda@1.4.0" has unmet peer dependency "aws-lambda@^0.1.2".
[4/4] Building fresh packages...
success Saved lockfile.
Done in 10.78s.

Added all functions & permissions of template email-password to graphcool.yml as comments
Added all types of template email-password to ./types.graphql as comments
Created ./src/email-password/:
  — authenticate.graphql
  — authenticate.ts
  — loggedInUser.graphql
  — loggedInUser.ts
  — signup.graphql
  — signup.ts

Please have a look in the graphcool.yml and types.graphql and uncomment the added template comments there.
```

The command results in some new additions:

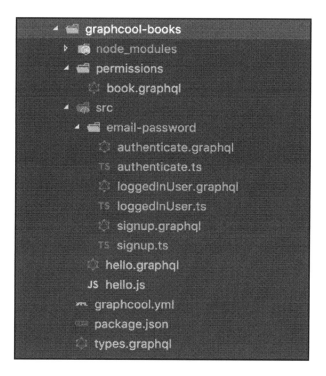

All the files under the `email-password` folder are new schema files, and the corresponding handler code files for the `signup`, `authenticate`, and `loggedInUser` resolver functions are defined in `graphcool.yml`.

 For the full code snippet, refer to `Code Snippets/Lesson 2` file.

2. In `graphcool.yml`, we will uncomment the new serverless functions for authentication:

```
...
# added by email-password template: (please uncomment)
signup:
  type: resolver
...
...
  type: resolver
```

```
schema: src/email-password/loggedInUser.graphql
handler:
  code: src/email-password/loggedInUser.ts
...
```

 For full code snippet, refer to `Code Snippets/Lesson 2` file.

3. A new `User` model is also added to `types.graphql`, but it is commented out. Since we already have such a model, we will simply merge the two and have an updated model. Our `types.graphql` file should look as follows after commenting out the dead code:

```
...
type User @model
{
  id: ID! @isUnique
...
  description: String!
  # Every relation also required a back-relation (to determine 1:1,
1:n or n:m)
  owner: User! @relation(name: "UserBooks")
}
...
```

 The different options that can be used for authentication are username and password, social login using Google/Facebook, and two-factor authentication.

Application Deployment

We can now deploy our application and test it out. Graphcool Cloud provides a free-tier service with three servers where we can deploy our application. We can also deploy our application locally using docker, but for this case, we will use the free Graphcool Cloud:

```
$ graphcool deploy
```

Take a look at this screenshot:

```
[94] → graphcool deploy
? Please choose the cluster you want to deploy to

shared-eu-west-1

? Please choose the target name prod
Creating service graphcool-books in cluster shared-eu-west-1... ✔
Bundling functions... 15.0s
Deploying... 3.3s

Success! Created the following service:

Types

  User
   + A new type with the name `User` is created.
   ├─ + A new field with the name `createdAt` and type `DateTime!` is created.
   ├─ + A new field with the name `updatedAt` and type `DateTime!` is created.
   ├─ + A new field with the name `name` and type `String` is created.
   ├─ + A new field with the name `dateOfBirth` and type `DateTime` is created.
   ├─ + A new field with the name `email` and type `String!` is created.
   └─ + A new field with the name `password` and type `String!` is created.
  Book
   + A new type with the name `Book` is created.
   ├─ + A new field with the name `createdAt` and type `DateTime!` is created.
   ├─ + A new field with the name `updatedAt` and type `DateTime!` is created.
   ├─ + A new field with the name `title` and type `String!` is created.
   └─ + A new field with the name `description` and type `String!` is created.

Relations

  UserBooks
   + The relation `UserBooks` is created. It connects the type `User` with the type `Book`.

Resolver Functions

  loggedInUser
   + A new resolver function with the name `loggedInUser` is created.
  authenticate
   + A new resolver function with the name `authenticate` is created.
  signup
   + A new resolver function with the name `signup` is created.
  hello
   + A new resolver function with the name `hello` is created.

Model Permissions

  User
   + A permission for the operation `create` is created.
   + A permission for the operation `read` is created.
  Book
   + A permission for the operation `create` is created.
   + A permission for the operation `read` is created.
   + A permission for the operation `update` is created.
   + A permission for the operation `delete` is created.
  UserBooks
   + A permission for the operation `connect` is created.

Here are your GraphQL Endpoints:

  Simple API:        https://api.graph.cool/simple/v1/cjddapjsi396n0127uit38boq
  Relay API:         https://api.graph.cool/relay/v1/cjddapjsi396n0127uit38boq
  Subscriptions API: wss://subscriptions.graph.cool/v1/cjddapjsi396n0127uit38boq
```

The information in the preceding screenshot details every aspect of our application. A new file called `.graphcoolrc` is also created with details about our deployment:

```
targets:
  prod: shared-eu-west-1/cjdd6us452bna0127vzi86zli
  default: prod
```

We can now access our application through the Simple API URL, either through the browser or desktop version of GraphQL Playground by running `graphcool playground`. We can click on the **Schema** button to see the available queries that were created automatically.

 While running this command, an error may arise saying `.graphqlconfig` file is not available in the provided `config` ..., just click the **OK** button to close it.

Take a look at this screenshot:

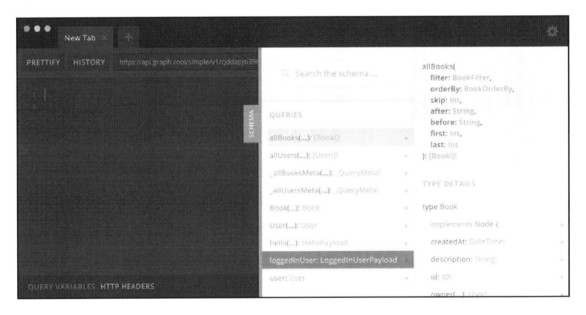

We can sign up a new user (`signupUser`), login (`authenticateUser`) with their credentials, and use the token provided to perform different operations. It is also important that we include the user ID in our response, since it is used as a link in creating a relationship between the user and their books. We will use this ID to set the `ownerID` when creating a book.

Creating (Signing Up) and Logging in (Authenticating) a User

Perform steps mentioned in this section to implement the sign up and authentication using mutations and variables.

The following screenshot shows how to signup a new user and authenticating to get a new token:

1. Create a mutation as follows:

```
mutation createNewUser($email: String!, $password: String!)
{
  signupUser(email:$email, password: $password)
  {
    id
  }
}
mutation login($email: String!, $password: String!)
{
  authenticateUser(email:$email, password: $password)
  {
    id
    token
  }
}
```

2. Create the variables as follows:

```
{
  "email": "brian@gmail.com",
  "password": "pass123"
}
```

Trying to create a new book will alert us about insufficient permissions. We need to use the token we got after signing in and also the `id` to set this as `ownerId`.

Generating the Insufficient Permissions Error with Missing Tokens

These steps will help you to generate insufficient permission error using mutations and variables.

The following screenshot shows the implementation of the mutation:

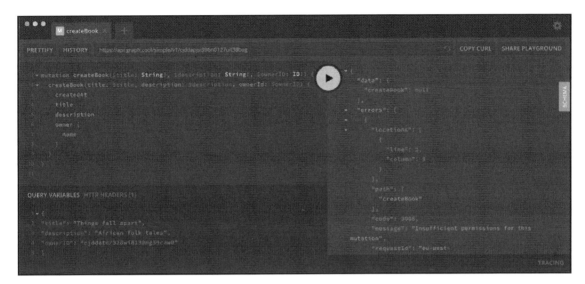

1. Create a mutation as follows:

```
mutation createBook($title: String!, $description: String!,
$ownerID: ID!)
{
  createBook(title: $title, description: $description,
  ownerId: $ownerID)
  {
    createdAt
    title
    description
    owner
    {
      name
    }
  }
}
```

2. Create the variables as follows:

```
{
  "title": "Things fall apart",
  "description": "African folk tales",
  "ownerID": "cjddat0r328wi0130ng39caw0"
}
```

To solve insufficient permission issue, we will include our token in the **HTTP HEADERS** section in the following format, after which we can play around with different queries in our playground:

```
{
    "Authorization": "Bearer Token"
}
```

You can create a book for an authenticated user (such as with the token provided) using the same mutation and variables we just used. Refer to this screenshot:

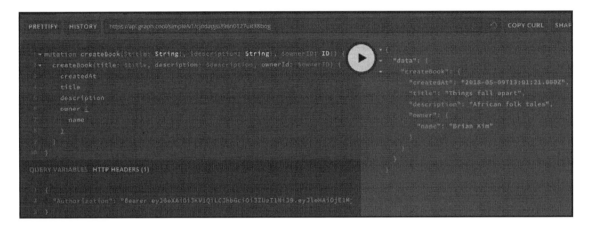

You can use Graphcool console to check the contents of the database, permissions, functions, and even open a GraphQL Playground in a hosted web interface. Look at this screenshot:

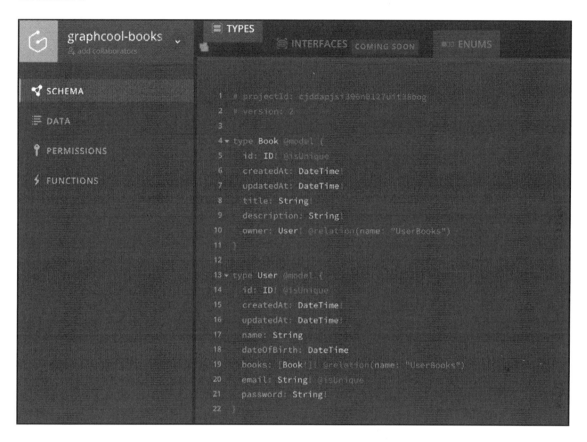

Prisma

Just like the Graphcool Framework, Prisma also converts our database into an API that we can access directly or extend its functionality, but has a slightly different approach. As you might have noticed in the previous section, Graphcool exposes a whole database and its methods. Prisma also exposes a whole database but with an additional application layer where we can dictate how to use the database methods.

Prisma also provides us with a Prisma CLI which we can use to initialize, manipulate, and deploy Prisma services:

```
$ npm install -g prisma@1.3.5 #Install Prisma CLI tool
```

We can initialize a new Prisma application using the CLI tool. The command will scaffold a new application inside a folder, `prisma-books`, using the recommended `node-basic` boilerplate:

```
$ prisma init prisma-books -b node-basic
```

Look at this screenshot:

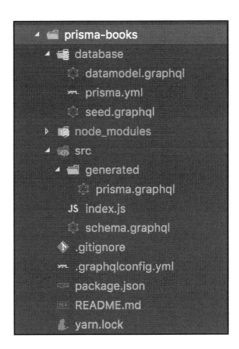

You will notice a difference in the folder structure between an application created by Graphcool CLI and Prisma CLI.

src Folder

The `src` folder holds the application schema (`schema.graphql`), auto-generated Prisma schema (`prisma.graphql`), and the JavaScript code that we can use to customize our API. The application schema defines the API that will be exposed to the client. It contains root schema definitions whose resolver functions are defined in `src/index.js`. The Prisma schema defines the CRUD API to our database. The file is auto-generated and updated on every deployment and should not be edited manually. The types exposed in the Prisma schema can be used to access database information through client methods in the application schema. Having the Prisma schema only will mean that client applications directly access the database and all methods, which is a bit too much since most developers will want to customize how and what information is accessed. This would also mean that we cannot implement alternative business logic around our CRUD API, like including authentication. The application schema gives us the ability to do that. The `src/index.js` file should look very familiar at this point, apart from a few new additions. It is a server built using `graphql-yoga`, which we have discussed in a previous section. We will notice a Prisma imported from `prisma-binding`. Schema binding enables us to reuse an existing GraphQL API, in this case, the database CRUD API. Let's examine the following code snippet:

```
...
const { GraphQLServer } = require('graphql-yoga')
const { Prisma } = require('prisma-binding')
...
...
    debug: true, // log all GraphQL queries & mutations
  }),
 }),
})
...
```

For complete code snippet, refer to `Code Snippets/Lesson 2` file. To learn more on schema binding, refer this URL `https://www.prisma.io/blog/graphql-schema-stitching-explained-schema-delegation-4c6caf468405/`.

Let's look at the highlighted part. When creating resolvers in a `graphql-yoga` server, context is the third parameter after the arguments. The preceding snippet is doing what we call **Schema Binding**; we are extending the auto-generated CRUD API and making it accessible through a property called `db` on the context object in the current application API. We will then be able to access the CRUD API methods (queries, mutations, and subscriptions) through `context.db`. The `typeDefs`, `endpoint`, and `secret` are like access configurations that enable the Prisma instance to access the CRUD API.

Database Folder

The database folder contains information related to the application database: the database model definition (`datamodel.graphql`), application configuration file (`prisma.yml`), and seed queries (`seed.graphql`):

- `datamodel.graphql`: Forms the basis on which our database will be created and the API generation of the methods in `src/generated/prisma.graphql`.
- `prisma.graphql`: A configuration file that defines the service name, deployment information, database model file name, and other information including authentication and database seed data.
- `seed.graphql`: Seed data is simply sample data that gets pre-populated into our database on initial deployment. This feature can be disabled by commenting out the seed part in `database/prisma.yml`.

`graphqlconfig.yml` is a configuration file based on `graphql-config` and is used by GraphQL Playground.

Application Development

Now that we have a clear understanding of a Prisma application ecosystem, we can continue building on our initial application with our own functionality.

Creating an Application Using Prisma

Perform the following steps to create an app and database section of our existing application using Prisma:

1. Create a `Book` model. By default, our application contains a Post type in `database/datamodel.graphql`. We will remove the `Post` model and create a `Book` model:

```
type Book
{
   id: ID! @unique
   createdAt:DateTime!
   updatedAt: DateTime!
   title: String! @unique
   description: String!
}
```

2. We will then run `prisma deploy` for changes to take place. This will also update `src/generated/prisma.yml` with methods that match the `Book` type. Trying to run the application at this point will result in errors since some sections are still trying to access the `Post` type, which we have removed. We can make some updates to correct this issue.

3. Create a resolver function to fetch all books:

```
File: src/index.js
...
/* Delete everything in the resolvers section and replace with the
following.*/
const resolvers =
{
  Query:
  {
    fetchAllBooks: (parent, args, ctx, info)=>
    {
/*
ctx.db.query.books references an auto-generated method in
src/generated/prisma.graphql which is enabled by prismabinding.
*/
      return ctx.db.query.books({}, info)
    }
  }
}
...
```

4. Import the `Book` type and use it to return a list of books. The comment-like import is enabled by `graphql-import`, which is a Prisma dependency:

```
File: src/schema.graphql
// Delete everything in the file and replace with the following.
...
# import Book from "./generated/prisma.graphql"
type Query
{
  fetchAllBooks: [Book!]!
}
...
```

We do not need to do a fresh deployment, since we have not made any changes to the model types inside `database/datamodel.graphql`.

5. To make our development easier, we will install `nodemon` and update the `start` script in `package.json` to use `nodemon`:

```
$ yarn global add nodemon #Alternatives: npm i nodemon -g
File: package.json
...
"start": "nodemon src/index.js" #Update start script to use nodemon
...
```

6. We can now run the application with `yarn dev`. This command starts up both a GraphQL server and GraphQL Playground connected to the server. The **GraphQL Playground** window has two sections on the far left.

Expected result: The command should automatically open the following windows:

- **app**: The **app** section represents client facing methods that we created that we can use in any client-side application. These schema methods use the auto-generated methods to communicate with the database.

 The desktop version of GraphQL Playground sometimes crashes randomly when started by Prisma. Frequent crashes can be avoided by copying the application URL into the browser and using the browser version.

- **database**: This section connects to the deployed database, and the schema shows the auto-generated queries, mutations, and subscriptions. It's also authenticated with a token already set in the headers. Take a look at this screenshot:

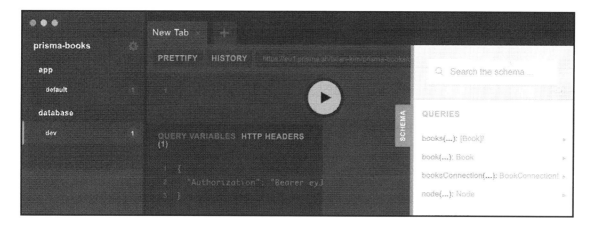

We can create a mutation to create a book under the `database-dev` section and fetch all books under the `app-default` section.

Creating a Book Record Directly in the Database Section

Perform the following steps to create a book record directly and fetch the books in the **database** section.

 It is not recommended to create a record directly in a real application.

The following screenshot shows how to create a book:

To create a book:

1. Define a mutation as follows:

```
mutation createBook($title: String!, $desc: String!)
{
  createBook(data: { title: $title, description: $desc})
  {
    title
    description
  }
}
```

2. Define the variables as follows:

```
{
   "title": "Da Vinci Code",
   "desc": "Crime, Thriller, Adventure and Misery genre"
}
```

Fetch all the books. Take a look at this screenshot:

3. Write the following query:

```
query fetchAllBooks
{
   fetchAllBooks
   {
      id
      title
      description
   }
}
```

4. Implement a book mutation and later on associate a book record with a user (as the owner) by creating a relation:

```
File: src/schema.graphql
// Include mutation for createBook
...
         info
      );
   }
   }
}
...
```

We can now create a book record in the **app** section. Take a look at this screenshot:

Define a mutation as follows:

```
mutation createNewBook($title: String!, $description: String!)
{
  createBook(title: $title, description: $description)
  {
    title
    description
  }
}
```

Define the variables as follows:

```
{
  "title": "Lost symbol",
  "description": "Dan Brown, thriller, adventure and misery"
}
```

Creating a Relationship with a User

We can now make a user an owner of a book by creating an owner field under the `Book` model type, and since we don't have a user, we will also have to create a `User` type in our model with a list of books. There's a slight difference between how we declare relations in Graphcool and relations in Prisma. Take a look at this code block:

```
File: database/datamodel.graphql
type Book
{
  id: ID! @unique
```

```
    createdAt:DateTime!
    updatedAt: DateTime!
    title: String! @unique
    description: String!
    owner: User # A book is owned by a User
}
type User
{
    id: ID! @unique
    email: String! @unique
    name: String!
    books: [Book!]! # A user can own several books
}
```

 The different relationships that exist in databases are one-to-one, one-to-many, and many-to-many.

When creating a new book, we can include a field that represents a user with any unique field: `id` or `email`. We need to redeploy the application for the changes to be applied to our database. Take a look at this screenshot:

```
[51] → prisma deploy
Deploying service `prisma-books` to stage `dev` on cluster `brian-kim/prisma-eu1` 495ms

Changes:

  User (Type)
  + Created type `User`
  + Created field `id` of type `GraphQLID!`
  + Created field `email` of type `String!`
  + Created field `name` of type `String!`
  + Created field `books` of type `[Relation!]!`
  + Created field `updatedAt` of type `DateTime!`
  + Created field `createdAt` of type `DateTime!`

  Book (Type)
  + Created field `owner` of type `Relation`

  BookToUser (Relation)
  + Created relation between Book and User
```

We can notice the information from the console indicating that a relationship has been created.

So far, we don't have any users, but we can create a user directly in the database section in GraphQL Playground and copy their ID and use it in creating a new book. Arguments for queries under the **database** section are put under a data object, unlike in the **app** section, where arguments are passed in directly. Take a look at this screenshot:

Define a mutation as follows:

```
mutation createNewUser($name: String!, $email: String!)
{
  createUser(data: { name: $name, email: $email})
  {
    id
  }
}
```

Define the variables as follows:

```
{
  "name": "Brian Kim",
  "email": "brian@kim.com"
}
```

The following screenshot shows how to create a book with an owner:

Creating a book with an owner

Define a mutation as follows:

```
mutation createBookWithAnOwner($title: String!, $desc: String!, $ownerID:
ID!){
createBook(data:
{
   title : $title, description: $desc,
   owner: { connect: { id: $ownerID}}})
   {
     title
     description
     owner
     {
       name
     }
   }
}
```

Define the variables as follows:

```
{
   "title": "Harry Porter",
   "desc": "Children's sci-fi and magic",
   "ownerID": "cjer89ma2000u0180m1f3qsgp"
}
```

The preceding mutation looks a bit complex. We will make it easier in the next section where we won't directly supply the ID of the owner on the client side but get it from the logged—in user details.

Looking at the schema description under the database, **dev** section, we can tell that we can connect a book to an owner (user) by supplying any unique value (ID or email) under connect object on owner:

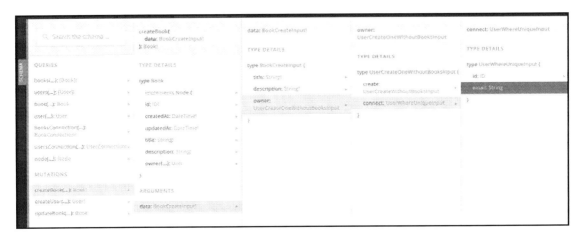

So far, that works fine, but looks a bit more complicated. We can make it better by allowing users to log in and automatically make a logged in user the owner of a book when they create one. This can be achieved by implementing authentication.

Authentication

In this section, we will create a sign up and login system after which we will issue a token to a user who has logged in successfully. The user can then use the token to perform different query and mutation operations. We will start by updating the user type in our model to include a password and re-deploy the application:

```
File: database/datamodel.graphql
...
type User
   {
   id: ID! @unique
   email: String! @unique
   name: String!
   books: [Book!]!
   password: String! # Include a password field
}
```

```
$ prisma deploy # Deploy changes
```

We will now require a user to sign up by providing their name, email, and password. We will leverage bcrypt.js (https://www.npmjs.com/package/bcryptjs) to encrypt and decrypt passwords and jsonwebtoken (https://www.npmjs.com/package/jsonwebtoken) to sign tokens and verify tokens.

 The authentication in this section is different than the authentication to the database. In this section, we implemented authentication for the application layer.

Updating Schema with loginUser and signupUser Methods

The following code shows you how to update schema with loginUser and signupUser methods:

```
File: src/schema.graphql
...
# Create a User type and AuthenticationPayload to be returned on login.
...
...
  signupUser(name: String!, email: String!, password: String!):User!
  loginUser(email: String!, password: String!):AuthenticationPayload!
}
```

We created a new user type when we could have imported it from the database/datamodel.graphql. This may seem unconventional, but there is a catch to importing it; if we import the user type, it will include the password field, which should not be exposed to the user at any point, even if it is encrypted. This enforces the whole concept of having an application layer on the existing database CRUD API.

The signupUser method returns a user object (type user) on success while the loginUser method returns a signed token and a user object (type user) combined as AuthenticationPayload on success.

Implementing the signupUser and loginUser Resolvers

We will need to install the required packages:

```
$ yarn add bcryptjs jsonwebtoken
File: src/index.js
...
// Import required packages
...
...
        token,
        user
      };
    }
  }
}
...
```

 For full code snippet, refer to `Code Snippets/Lesson 2` file.

The preceding snippet is pretty straightforward, providing sign up and login functionality. We are also utilizing `async` since the operations involved in hashing passwords and querying the database API are asynchronous. Take a look at this screenshot:

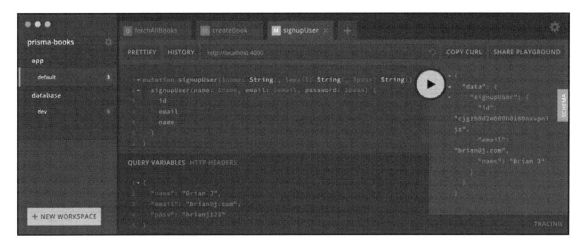

Define a mutation as follows:

```
mutation signupUser($name: String!, $email: String!, $pass: String!)
{
  signupUser(name: $name, email: $email, password: $pass)
  {
    id
    email
    name
  }
}
```

Define a query as follows:

```
{
  "name": "Brian J",
  "email": "brian@j.com",
  "pass": "brianj123"
}
```

We can then login using the preceding credentials to get a token which we should copy somewhere to use for future operations. Take a look at this screenshot:

Define a mutation as follows:

```
mutation loginUser($email: String!, $pass: String!)
{
  loginUser(email: $email, password: $pass)
  {
    token,
    user
```

```
      {
        id
        email
      }
    }
  }
}
```

Define a query as follows:

```
{
  "email": "brian@j.com",
  "pass": "brianj123"
}
```

For now, a user can create an account and login, but we need to ensure that a logged-in user can create a book record and that the record is associated with them.

Associating a User with a Book Record

This step will involve retrieving a `userId` from the token, and then using it to create a book record. Since the token is attached to the header, we can access it through the `request` object on the context parameter in the resolver functions. We will then modify our `createBook` mutation to include the owner:

```
File: src/index.js
...
// Verify token and retrieve userId from token
...
      },
      info
    );
  },
...
}
...
```

 For full code snippet, refer to `Code Snippets/Lesson 2` file.

With the preceding modifications, we can make less complex queries from the client, since the connect part has been handled on the server side. Take a look at this screenshot:

```
QUERY VARIABLES   HTTP HEADERS (1)

1  {
2      "bookTitle": "GraphQL Intro",
3      "bookDesc": "Beginner to intermediate level GraphQL course"
4  }
```

The following screenshot shows client side querying:

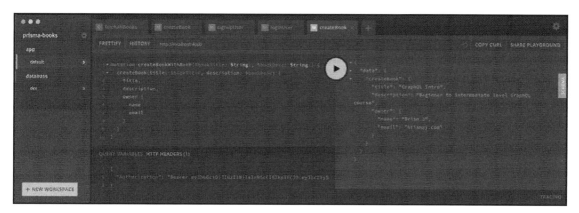

Define a mutation as follows:

```
mutation createBookWithAuth($bookTitle: String!, $bookDesc: String!)
{
  createBook(title: $bookTitle, description: $bookDesc)
  {
    title,
    description,
    owner
    {
      name
      email
    }
  }
}
```

Define the variables as follows:

```
{
    "bookTitle": "GraphQL Intro",
    "bookDesc": "Beginner to intermediate level GraphQL course"
}
```

Define the HTTP headers as follows:

```
{
    "Authorization": "Bearer Token"
}
```

We need to include the token in the header of the preceding request. Failure to include it will result in an `Authentication Failed` error, as follows:

Activity: Deploying the Application Locally on Docker

Aim

To deploy the application locally on the Docker.

 This activity is an extension of the previous application under Prisma. To complete this activity, you'll need to have completed the application under the *Prisma* section. If you are missing any code sections, the GitHub folder contains all the functioning code for the Prisma section. This activity will also require Docker to be running. Docker can be started on macOS platforms by searching for Docker in the Launchpad and clicking on it, or simply by going through the Spotlight.

Scenario

Consider being in a larger development team that has single staging and single production environments, but every developer needs to test their application locally in a uniform environment (Docker). This will mean deploying our application locally on Docker.

Steps for Completion

1. Navigate to the application folder (`prisma-books`) and start a local development cluster by running the following command:

   ```
   $ prisma local start
   ```

2. Run the Prisma cluster command's list to confirm if a local cluster was created.

3. We can then deploy the application locally by running `prisma deploy --interactive`. This will show a list of existing clusters. Use the arrow keys to select `local`.

4. We need to update out application to use the local database on Docker. Open the project folder in a new Terminal and run the command `prisma info` to get the URL of the service.

5. Copy the HTTPS URL and update `src/index.js` by setting the endpoint section under `server` to the HTTPS URL:

   ```
   const server = new GraphQLServer({
     typeDefs: "./src/schema.qraphql",
     resolvers,
     context: req => ({
       ...req,
   ```

```
      db: new Prisma({
        typeDefs: "src/generated/prisma.graphql",
        endpoint: "http://localhost:4466/prisma-books/dev",
        // the endpoint of the Prisma DB service
        secret: "mysecret123",
        // specified in database/prisma.yml
        debug: true
        // log all GraphQL queries & mutations
      })
    })
  });
```

6. We can then run our application using the `yarn dev` command. This should open the **graphql-playground** window.

Due to the early development nature of Prisma, you may experience some issues carrying out the preceding activity. In case running the `prisma deploy-interactive` command does not present a set of cluster options, open the application folder and inside `database/prisma.yml`, comment out the `cluster` section.

7. To reset all the service data, run the following command:

`prisma local nuke`

8. In the case of an error that states `'ECONNRESET': request to http://localhost:4466/cluster failed, reason: socket hang up`, list the available Docker containers using the `docker ps` command and stop the Prisma container using `docker stop [OPTIONS] CONTAINER [CONTAINER...]`.

Prisma has since created a Prisma Cloud service, similar to Graphcool Cloud, where we can visualize our data and models. To browse your data using Prisma Cloud, you can sign up using an email and password or GitHub. This service is not available for applications locally deployed on Docker. Prisma Cloud also provides the GraphQL Playground, where we can query and mutate our data. The interface provides direct access to the Database API and not our own built client API. To open Prisma Cloud directly, upgrade your Prisma version to 1.8.0, using the `npm i -g prisma` command inside the Prisma console.

Define the mutation as follows:

```
mutation createNewBook($title: String!, $description: String!)
{
  createBook(data: { title: $title, description: $description})
  {
    id
    createdAt
    updatedAt
    title
    description
  }
}
```

Define the variables as follows:

```
{
  "title": "The Legend of the Seeker",
  "description": "Book description"
}
```

Summary

In this chapter, we covered how we can make our server respond to requests in real time. We also covered third-party development tools by Graphcool that have made learning and implementation of GraphQL very easy. Finally, we learned about the different entities of a GraphQL application and the base concepts involving queries and mutations and different ways of writing them.

In the next chapter, we will cover how to access a simple web-based application to access queries instead of writing them manually. We will also cover how we can have our application interface update in real time and how to make optimistic UI updates.

3
Integrating GraphQL with Server-Side Applications Using the Apollo Client

In the previous chapters, we were testing all our server applications using GraphQL and GraphQL Playground. The two tools work well in the development environment, but for real-world applications, we need a real user-friendly client application where we don't write queries directly but interact with a simple web-based application.

In this chapter, we are going to use the Apollo Client together with the view layer implementation for React called React Apollo. It is a flexible GraphQL client which is used to build React applications. We will cover how to use a simple web-based application to access queries instead of writing them manually. We will also cover how we can have our application interface update in real time and how to make optimistic UI updates.

By the end of this chapter, you will be able to:

- Set up a simple GraphQL client using React JS and the Apollo Client
- Connect a client application to the server using GraphQL
- Update user interfaces using optimistic updates

Setting up a React Client Application

In this section, we will be setting up the React client application. React client application helps us to build a user-friendly client-side application for GraphQL.

Perform the following steps to set up a React application using GitHub:

1. Clone the boilerplate from GitHub using one of the following commands:
   - To clone with SSH, type the following command:

     ```
     git clone -b graphql-boilerplate
     git@github.com:kimobrian/React-Setup.git
     ```

   - To clone with HTTPS, use the following command:

     ```
     git clone -b graphql-boilerplate
     https://github.com/kimobrian/React-Setup.git
     ```

   This will create a directory, `React-Setup`, with the following contents:

   ```
   ├── app
   │   ├── app.js
   │   ├── components
   │   │   └── BooksComponent.jsx
   │   ├── config
   │   │   └── routes.js
   │   └── index.tmpl.html
   ├── package.json
   ├── webpack.config.js
   └── webpack.production.config.js
   ```

2. Navigate into the folder using `cd React-Setup`.
3. Install the required packages with the following commands, depending on whether you are using YARN or npm as the package manager:
   - Using npm: `npm i`
   - Using YARN: `yarn`

4. We can test our application by running either the `yarn start` or `npm start` command. We will then navigate to the browser using the URL `http://localhost:7700/`.

Expected result: We should see the following interface in our browser window:

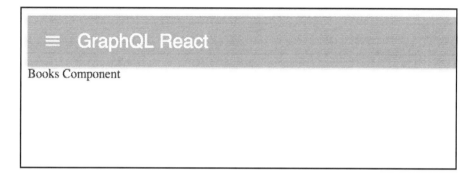

Fetching a List of Books

Our server application stores a list of books that we should be able to display in our client application. You may recall from `Chapter 2`, *Querying Real-Time Data*, that we had the following while fetching all books:

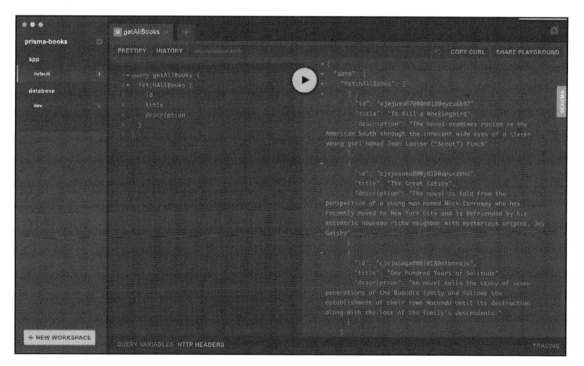

ed to translate this into a real application by utilizing Apollo Client to
the implementation.

Using Apollo Client

Apollo Client is the ultra-flexible, GraphQL client for React, JavaScript, and native
platforms. Apollo Client automatically takes care of a lot of implementations that would be
complex and difficult to implement. It takes care of all requests, including tracking loading
states and errors. It also offers a cache to track data locally and increases the speed of the
application with very little configuration.

> The application from our last chapter must be up and running for this part
> to be completed successfully. This application will work for either the
> locally hosted server application on Docker, or the one deployed on
> Prisma Cloud. Get the URLs of the backend service for use with the client.

Linking a React Application

Perform the following steps to link a React application with GraphQL using Apollo Client
and `react-apollo`:

1. Install the required packages, which we will explain at a later stage by running
   the following command:

   ```
   yarn add apollo-client apollo-cache-inmemory apollo-link-http
   react-apollo graphql-tag graphql
   ```

2. Connect the root application with Apollo Client.
3. Update the `app/config/routes.js` file to the following:

   ```
   import React from 'react';
   import ReactDOM from 'react-dom';
   import { BrowserRouter, Route, Switch } from 'react-router-dom';
   ```

   Replace the existing `BooksComponent` import with `BooksComponentWithData`.
   We will define `BooksComponentWithData` in the next step:

   ```
   import BooksComponentWithData from '../components/BooksComponent';
   import MuiThemeProvider from 'material-ui/styles/MuiThemeProvider';
   import AppBar from 'material-ui/AppBar';
   import { ApolloClient } from 'apollo-client';
   import { HttpLink } from 'apollo-link-http';
   ```

```
import { InMemoryCache } from 'apollo-cache-inmemory';
import { ApolloProvider } from 'react-apollo';
```

- Create a GraphQL client using Apollo Client:

```
const client = new ApolloClient({
```

- Copy the following URL from the GraphQL Playground app section. It will be different if you're using Prisma Cloud:

```
//The link is used to get GraphQL results over a network
using HTTP fetch
link: new HttpLink({ uri: 'http://localhost:4000' }),
/*
The InMemoryCache replaces Redux used in Apollo Client 1.x.
This acts a store to hold application state
*/
cache: new InMemoryCache()
});
const AppBarComponent = () => <AppBar title="GraphQL React"
/>;
const routes = (
  <MuiThemeProvider>
    <ApolloProvider client={client}>
      <BrowserRouter>
        <div>
          <AppBarComponent />
          <Switch>
```

- Copy the following URL from the GraphQL Playground app section. It will be different if you're using Prisma Cloud:

```
            <Route exact path="/" component={
BooksComponentWithData } />
          </Switch>
        </div>
      </BrowserRouter>
    </ApolloProvider>
  </MuiThemeProvider>
);
export default routes;
```

We have added some new packages in our application. Let's understand what they actually do:

- `ApolloClient` is the center of using GraphQL in the application. It manages all of the data so that we can focus on features. We use it to create a GraphQL client by supplying a URI of our server application. We also pass it a cache option, which is set to `InMemoryCache`. This is a normalized data store for GraphQL data that is equivalent to a Redux store in React.
- Apollo can be used anywhere in our React component hierarchy with the help of `ApolloProvider`. It's the equivalent of the context provider for React or the provider from Redux. It allows you to access the client from anywhere in your component tree by wrapping the React app and placing the client on the context. This component helps to share the React Apollo functionality to all the other components in the application without passing it explicitly.

From this point on, any components rendered under our main application component have access to the GraphQL data.

4. Update the `BooksComponent` to make GraphQL requests:

In this step, we are going to make a request to fetch the existing list of books and display them. Update `app/components/BooksComponent.jsx` to the following:

```
import React, { Component } from 'react';
import { List, ListItem } from 'material-ui/List';
import CircularProgress from 'material-ui/CircularProgress';
import { Card, CardActions, CardHeader, CardText } from
'material-
...
const BooksComponentWithData =
graphql(getBooksQuery)(BooksComponent);
export default BooksComponentWithData;
```

For full code snippets, refer to the `Code Snippets/Lesson3.graphql` file.

We have also added some new information in the `BooksComponent`. Let's see exactly what is happening.

We first import some components from `material-ui` for faster UI design. We also import some functions that are specific to GraphQL:

- `gql` is a JavaScript template literal tag. Its functionality is to parse the GraphQL query strings into the standard GraphQL AST. This may then be consumed by Apollo Client methods. We have used this function to create a query, `fetchAllBooks`, to return all books.
- `graphql` from `react-apollo` connects our `BooksComponent` to the GraphQL API. We can now access data that is fetched inside the component.

When a GraphQL request is made to fetch data, the data is included in the `props` and contains an `error` section, `loading`, and the actual data (`books`):

```
let { error, loading, books } = this.props.data;
```

We can use these variables to show the correct UI. For instance, we are showing a circular spinner when loading is `true`. We see this loader when the application starts loading and then it disappears to show the actual data. We then display the list of books (title and description) using the `map` function:

5. Run the application using the `yarn start` command and navigate to the browser using the client URL `http://localhost:7700/`.

Expected output: The browser window should appear as follows. This is the exact list of books we got in GraphQL Playground previously:

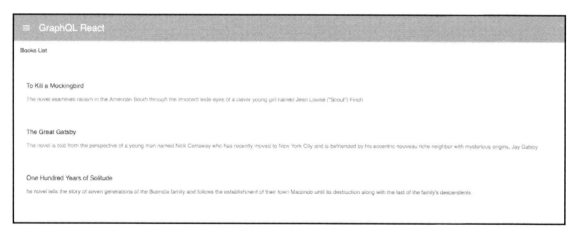

Authentication

To implement authentication, a user logs in using the right credentials and the server sends back a **JSON Web Token (JWT)** token. We save the JWT token in local storage and send the token along every request. Once the server verifies the authenticity of the token, it can then carry out the requested operation.

Activity: Implementing Register and Login Functionalities

Aim

To add *Register* and *Login* sections in our application for new and existing users.

Scenario

While building our application, we can decide whether anyone can see the list of books, but only registered users can create new books and update existing books. Therefore, we need to update our application to have *Register* sections for new users and *Login* sections for existing users.

 We already have this functionality in our server-side application, so we are just providing a client-side implementation for the same.

Steps for Completion

1. Create a UI for *Login* and *Register* sections. In this step, we create two components, one for login and the other for registration:

   - Create the `app/components/Authentication.jsx` folder, which will hold the *Login* and *Register* components, and paste in the following code snippet:

```
import React, { Component } from 'react';
import { Tabs, Tab } from 'material-ui/Tabs';
import { Card, CardText } from 'material-ui/Card';
...
  },
  center:
  {
    textAlign: 'center'
  }
};
```

 For full code snippets, refer to the `Code Snippets/Lesson3.graphql` file.

   - The preceding code snippet creates a skeleton of the `Login` and `Register` components and renders them with an `Authentication` component.
   - Update the `Login` component to the following:

```
class Login extends Component
{
  constructor(props)
  {
...
...
        <br />
        <RaisedButton label="Login" primary={true}
onClick={this.loginUser} />
      </div>
    );
  }
}
```

The preceding snippet creates a `Login` interface with two input fields for an email and a password. The component also has error handlers that will show errors when empty fields are submitted on login.

- Update `app/config/routes.js` to include a route to render the `Authentication` component.

```
import React from 'react';
import ReactDOM from 'react-dom';
import { BrowserRouter, Route, Switch } from 'reactrouter-dom';
...
...
    </ApolloProvider>
  </MuiThemeProvider>
);
export default routes;
```

- Run the application using `yarn start` and navigate to the browser using the URL `http://localhost:7700/login`. We should see the following interface that shows an error message when the password field is empty:

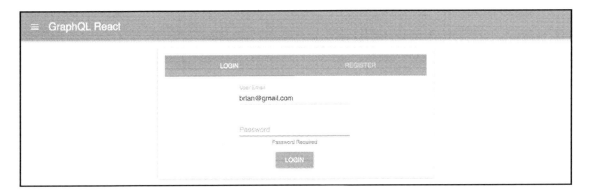

For full code snippets, refer to the `Code Snippets/Lesson3.graphql` file.

- Update the `Register` component to the following:

```
class Register extends Component {
  constructor(props)   {
...
        <RaisedButton label="Register" primary
onClick={ this.registerNewUser }/>
      </div>
    );}
}
```

- The preceding code does pretty much the same as the `Login` component, in that it creates a UI and shows error messages.
- Inside the current project directory, run the application using `yarn start` and navigate to the browser using the URL `http://localhost:7700/login`. The following interface should appear when the **REGISTER** tab is clicked. Play around with the fields to see the different errors:

Implementing User Registration

Now that we have the interface, we should hook it up with GraphQL to register users using the mutation `signupUser(...)`.

 We are still using the GraphQL server application from the previous chapter under the Prisma section. *Activity: Deploying the Application Locally on Docker* from Chapter 2, *Querying Real-Time Data* can also be used for this application. The only difference is that the application in the activity is hosted on Docker while the application under the Prisma topic is hosted on Prisma cloud.

We need to create a query so that we can create a new user and link it with the `Register` component in order to access data inside the component. We will accomplish this by importing the required methods, creating the query, and linking it to the component as follows:

1. Create a user signup query and connect it to the `Register` component.
2. Update `app/components/Authentication.jsx` with the highlighted information:

```
// ... other imports
import RaisedButton from 'material-ui/RaisedButton';
//Import the required functions
...
            </CardText>
          </Card>
        </div>
      );
    }
  }
```

In the preceding snippet, we are creating a query that creates a new user. We then call the method when the **REGISTER** button is clicked. With the preceding code, we can run the application using `yarn start` and try to register a new user. After saving a new user, we should see the logs in the browser console, similar to the following:

```
User created Successfully: ▼ {data: {…}} ◉          Authentication.jsx:122
                           ▼ data:
                             ▼ user:
                                 email: "joshua@king.com"
                                 id: "cjerhzd9b00210180djn8aflg"
                                 name: "Joshua King"
                                 __typename: "User"
                              ▶ __proto__: Object
                          ▶ __proto__: Object
                      ▶ __proto__: Object
```

Trying to feed in an existing user email will result in an error on the console:

```
⊗ ▶ GraphQL error: A unique constraint would be violated on User.     Authentication.jsx:130
    Details: Field name = email
```

Implementing User Login

Now that we can register a user, we need to get a token by logging into our application using our email and password.

We will begin by creating a login mutation and then connecting it to the `Login` component. We will also render the connected component inside the `Authentication` component instead of the default `Login` component.

When the LOGIN button is clicked, the login request will be made, and as a result, we will get an authentication token. We will then save the token in our local storage and use it for subsequent requests.

Update the code in `app/components/Authentication.jsx` as follows. We are only updating sections of code and not everything:

```
const loginUser = gql`
  mutation login($email: String!, $password: String!) {
    user: loginUser(email: $email, password: $password) {
      token
  ...
  ...
  </Tab>
  //... skipped code
  }
}
```

We can run the application using `yarn start` and navigate to the browser using the `http://localhost:7700/login` URL, and then try to log in. After successful login, in our browser's Developer Tools section under **Local Storage**, we should see that the token has been saved:

Key	Value
authToken	eyJhbGciOiJIUzI1NiIsInR5cCI6IkpXVCJ9.eyJ1c2VySWQ...

⊗ ▶Error: GraphQL error: Invalid password   Authentication.jsx:48

> You can access Developer Tools by right-clicking anywhere in the browser window and selecting **Inspect Element**. They can then navigate to the **Application** section which has **Local Storage**.

Now that we can register a new user, log in, and get a token, we can use that token to create a new book record using the `createBook` mutation.

Creating the UI for a New Book with Validations

To create a new book, we will make a new component and make the component only accessible to logged in users. This means that unauthorized users cannot create new books.

Creating a New Book

Perform the following steps to create a new book form with proper validations:

1. Create a `NewBook` component. Create a file called `app/components/NewBook.jsx` and paste the following code inside it:

```
// File app/components/NewBook.jsx
import React, { Component } from 'react';
import { Card, CardHeader, CardText } from 'material-ui/Card';
import TextField from 'material-ui/TextField';
...
...
            </div>
          </CardText>
        </Card>
```

```
      </div>
    );
  }
}
export default NewBook;
```

The preceding snippet simply creates an interface for our component, which we will look at shortly. It also handles errors in case of missing values and has a link to the list of existing books.

2. Create functions to control login and logout. We need utility functions that will help us log out of the application and also check whether we are logged in or not:

   1. Install `jwt-decode` to help get information from the token using the following command inside our current project directory:

      yarn add jwt-decode

   2. Create a file called `app/utils.jsx` with a `logout` function and another function to check if a user is logged in, and paste the following code:

      ```
      //File: app/utils.jsx
      import React from 'react';
      import { Redirect } from 'react-router-dom';
      ...
      ...
      };
      module.exports = { isLoggedIn, logout };
      ```

3. Update the routes to render the `NewBook` component. Now, we need to update our `app/config/routes.jsx` function to include a route to render the `NewBook` component. This route will also be protected so that only logged in users can access it. We will also create a logout button that will be visible when a user is logged in. Apart from this, we will include a route that defaults to the `Login` page if a nonexistent route is supplied in the address bar:

   ```
   // File: app/config/routes.jsx
   import React from 'react';
   import ReactDOM from 'react-dom';
   // Import the Redirect component
   import { BrowserRouter, Route, Switch, Redirect } from
   'reactrouter-dom';
   // ... skipped imports
   ...
   ...
         </div>
   ```

```
          </BrowserRouter>
        </ApolloProvider>
      </MuiThemeProvider>
  );
  export default routes;
```

4. Update the `Login` component inside `app/components/Authentication.jsx` to redirect to the page with existing books after successful login. Inside this file, update the `loginUser` method under the `Login` component to the following:

 For full code snippets, refer to the `Code Snippets/Lesson 3`.

```
// app/components/Authentication.jsx
// ... code before
loginUser()
{
  this.setState({ emailError: '', passwordError: '' });
...
...
    this.setState({ email: '', password: '', emailError: 'Invalid
Login Credentials' });
    console.error('Error:', err.message);
  });
}
// ... code after
```

5. Update the `app/components/BooksComponent.jsx` file to include a link stating `CREATE A NEW BOOK` for logged in users. This will redirect them to the page with the form to create new books:

```
// File: app/components/BooksComponent.jsx
//... skipped imports
import { Link } from 'react-router-dom';
import FlatButton from 'material-ui/FlatButton';
...
...
            <List>
               //... skipped code
            </List>
          </CardText>
        </Card>
      );
    }
}
```

6. Run the application inside the application directory and navigate to the browser using the URL `http://localhost:7700/login`. We should be able to login and be redirected to the page with the existing list of books. The page has a link called `CREATE A NEW BOOK` that should send users to the page so that they can create new books.

The following screenshots shows the login page:

Book list page:

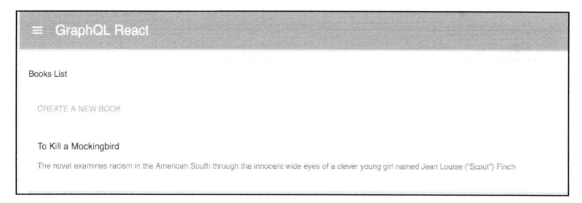

Create new book page:

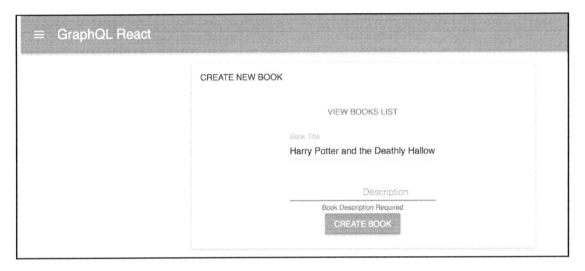

So far, the **CREATE NEW BOOK** form does not do anything important apart from validate the forms.

Integrating GraphQL into the NewBook Component

Up to this point, all we need is to integrate GraphQL into our `NewBook` component to do actual book creation using the `createBook` mutation.

 Redux, MobX, NgRx, flux, and Jumpsuit are the state management libraries and methods in the JavaScript ecosystem.

In this section, we are going to connect our `NewBook` component to GraphQL. This will enable us to create new book records.

We are also going to integrate optimistic UI features that will enable our user interface to update without any delays. The optimistic patches are stored in a separate place in the cache, so once the actual mutation returns, the relevant optimistic update is automatically thrown away and replaced with the real result.

Our application is going to store the data in an `InMemoryCache` and retrieve it for later use to avoid unnecessary network requests.

The `InMemoryCache` is an equivalent of state management libraries like `Redux`.

Linking the NewBook Component to GraphQL

Perform the following steps to create a book for redirecting to a page with lists of books:

1. Update `app/components/NewBook.jsx` to connect it to the GraphQL client. In this part, we are going to initialize the `createBook` mutation and link it with the `NewBook` component. Update `app/components/NewBook.jsx` with the following changes:

```
// File app/components/NewBook.jsx
//... Skipped imports
import gql from 'graphql-tag';
import { graphql } from 'react-apollo';
...
...
      })
    })
}) (NewBook);
/*
Export the connected component
*/
export default NewBookComponentWithData;
```

2. Update `app/components/BooksComponent.jsx`. In this section, we going to make `getBooksQuery` available outside this module by exporting it. Instead of rewriting the query in the `NewBook` component, we are going to simply export and reuse it. The only update is going to be adding the `export` keyword to the query:

```
//...skipped code
export const getBooksQuery = gql`
//... skipped query content
`;
//...skipped code
```

3. Update the client to include the authentication token:
    - Since the mutation to create a new book record needs an authenticated user, we need to attach authorization headers to the request and render the connected `NewBookComponentWithData` component instead of the initial `NewBook` component. We also need our cache to always maintain up-to-date data by setting a cache-and-network fetch policy. With this policy, the Apollo Client will query the server, but

return data from the cache while the server request is pending, and later update the result when the server response has come back. We will also need to clear out our cache on logout by calling `client.resetStore()`.

- We will create a middleware with Apollo Links that will let us modify the request before sending it to the server by adding an authorization header. We will use `apollo-link-context`, which will allow us to set the context of the request:

  ```
  yarn add apollo-link-context
  ```

  - Update `app/config/routes.js` to create a context and attach it to the Apollo Client, and render the connected `NewBook` component (`NewBookComponentWithData`):

  ```
  // File: app/config/routes.js
  //...skipped imports
  import NewBookComponentWithData from
  '../components/NewBook';
  import FlatButton from 'material-ui/FlatButton';
  ...
  ...
          <Route path="*" component={Authentication} />
        </Switch>
  //... skipped code
  );
  export default routes;
  ```

 For full code snippets, refer to the `Code Snippets/Lesson 3`.

4. We can then test out our application by navigating into the application folder and starting the application with `yarn start`. We can then navigate to the create new book page, like in the previous example. Then, we can create a book in the form. This will create a book and redirect us to the page with the list of books with the new book on the list.

Testing the Whole Application Workflow

Perform the following steps to test the creation of a new book record:

1. While the application is running, we can log in by navigating to the **LOGIN** page, where we can input the correct login credentials. We can always register if we don't have an account:

2. After successful login, we will be ushered to a page with a list of existing books:

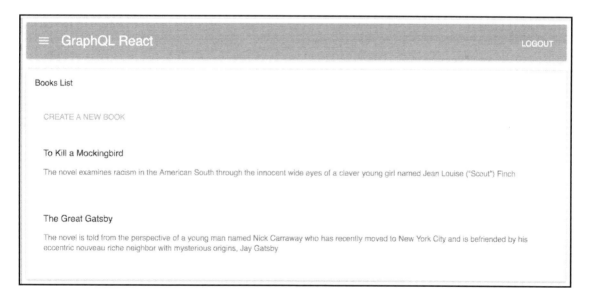

3. Using the **CREATE A NEW BOOK** link, we can navigate to a page where we can create a new book by supplying a title and description, and click on the **CREATE BOOK** button:

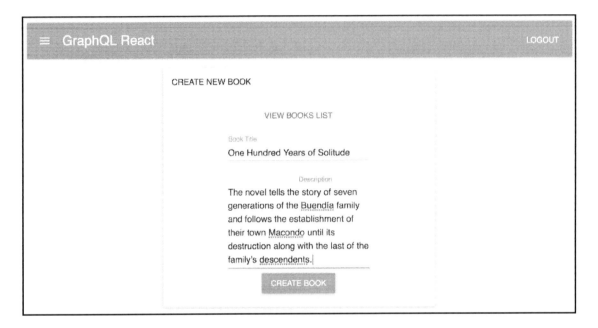

4. We should be redirected back to the list of books with the new book record available. Notice the third item in the following screenshot:

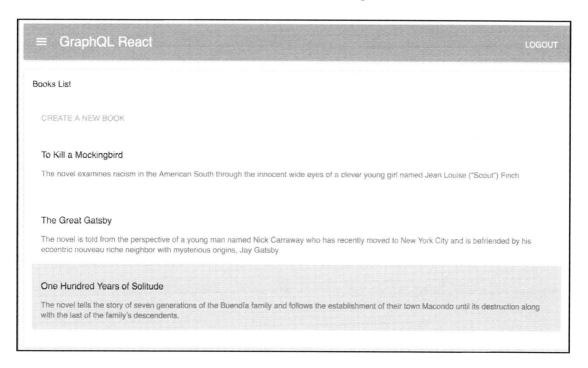

Summary

In this chapter, we have covered an essential part of any application; creating interactive, user-friendly interfaces. We have explored how we can integrate GraphQL functionality inside a React application using Apollo Client, react-apollo, and other packages. We have covered how the client cache works and how we can connect components to retrieve data from the cache and even update the cache. We have also included optimistic UI, a feature that allows us to update the UI with hopes that the requests will be successful but revert on error.

This, combined with all the previous chapters, brings to an end a very detailed understanding of GraphQL and its features. Most features demonstrated are from beginner to an intermediate level, which will make it very easy for the learners to pick up advanced features.

Other Products You May Enjoy

If you enjoyed this book, you may be interested in these other products by Packt:

Learning GraphQL and Relay

Samer Buna

ISBN: 978-1-78646-575-7

- Understand what problem GraphQL solves and how it differs from traditional REST architectures
- Create a GraphQL server
- Develop modular and maintainable GraphQL code
- Grasp how to define GraphQL mutations
- Comprehend how to define GraphQL queries
- Modify a GraphQL server to be Relay-compliant
- Develop a Relay client-side application with ReactJS that consumes a GraphQL endpoint

Hands-on GraphQL for Better RESTful Web Services [Video]
Ashwin Hegde

ISBN: 978-1-78899-562-7

- Exploit the benefits of using GraphQL for better RESTful web service development
- Explore the architecture and the use cases of GraphQL
- Code with GraphQL routes for the server
- Practice and work with schema construction
- Use GraphQL tools to fetch and introspect your data
- Learn tips and tricks to easily fetch data using queries
- Update data and display data for performing CRUD operations
- Authentication

Leave a review - let other readers know what you think

Please share your thoughts on this book with others by leaving a review on the site that you bought it from. If you purchased the book from Amazon, please leave us an honest review on this book's Amazon page. This is vital so that other potential readers can see and use your unbiased opinion to make purchasing decisions, we can understand what our customers think about our products, and our authors can see your feedback on the title that they have worked with Packt to create. It will only take a few minutes of your time, but is valuable to other potential customers, our authors, and Packt. Thank you!

Index

Made in the USA
Middletown, DE
28 February 2019